240/1000

**SPECIAL FIRST EDITION
AUTHOR COPY**

Simple Psychology

SIMPLE LIVING IN A COMPLICATED WORLD

by

Tom Reilly

Published by

MOTIVATION PRESS

St. Louis, MO

*To Amanda, Paul and Andrew Reilly
my children.
I love you.
Thank you for helping me see the world
through your eyes.*

Library of Congress Cataloging-in-Publication Data

Reilly, Thomas P.

Simple Psychology

Other Books by Tom Reilly:
Value Added Selling Techniques™
Value Added Sales Management
Value Added Customer Service
Selling Smart

Copyright©, 1996 by Tom Reilly
Library of Congress Catalog Card Number: 96-094359
International Standard Book Number: 0-944448-11-9

All rights reserved. No part of this publication may be reproduced or transmitted in any form or by any means, electronic or mechanical including photocopy, recording, or any information retrieval system without permission in writing from the publisher or Tom Reilly, c/o Motivation Press, 171 Chesterfield Industrial Blvd., Chesterfield, MO 63005

Printed in the United States of America by Motivation Press.

Contents

Introduction   1

SECTION ONE - What's Really Important In Life

1. Wake-Up Call   5
2. Success Is The Quality Of Your Journey   7
3. Balance Your Life   9
4. Less Is More   12
5. Happiness   14
6. Unconditional Love   16
7. Parent's Prayer   17

SECTION TWO - The World Is A Big Sand Box

8. Life Is Bigger Than Me   19
9. Can I Make A Difference   21
10. Can I *Really* Make A Difference   23
11. Leave A Little Bigger Woodpile
    Than The One You Found!   25
12. We Is Greater Than Me   27

SECTION THREE - Positive Attitude

13. Making Lemonade   29
14. Positive Mental Programming   31
15. Believe And Behave   33
16. Burdens And Blessings   35
17. Adversity Brings Out The Best In You   37
18. It's Not So Much What Happens To You . . .   39

SECTION FOUR - Focused Effort

19. Focusing   42
20. Make A Commitment To Commit   44
21. Delayed Gratification: Patient Persistence   46
22. Perfection Versus Excellence   48
23. P.R.I.D.E.   50

SECTION FIVE - Positive Action

24. Dream Big Dreams   52
25. So Many Dreams, So Little Time   54
26. Initiative   56
27. Everyone Needs A Push   58
28. Play Hard, Have Fun, And Never Quit   59

SECTION SIX - Personal Performance

29. How To Compete   62
30. Phenoms and Fundamentalists   64
31. The Performance Formula   66
32. Develop Good Habits   68
33. Are You A High Achiever?   70

SECTION SEVEN - Risk Is A Four-Letter Word

34. Take A Risk   73
35. If It Ain't Broke, Don't Fix It! Why Not?   75
36. It's Easier To Ask Forgiveness Than Permission   76
37. Expect Buffeting Along The Way   78
38. The Fear of Failure   80
39. The Fear of Success   83
40. On The Vanguard Of Change   85

SECTION EIGHT - How To Get More Out Of Life

41. Act Like You're Worth It   87
42. Avoid Early Mental Retirement   89
43. Blast Out of Your Comfort Zone   90
44. Low-Hanging Fruit   93
45. Do You Add Value Or Cost?   95
46. Positive Action: Get Busy   96
47. There's No Traffic Jam On The Extra Mile   98
48. The Grass Is Always Greener   100

SECTION NINE - Motivation

49. Confusing Values With Motivation   103
50. Intrinsic Versus Extrinsic Motivation   105
51. Money And Motivation   107
52. Is Your Job Motivating?   109
53. Real-World Motivation   111

SECTION TEN - Treat Yourself Right

54. Celebrate Your Successes	114
55. Create Your Own Luck	117
56. Cut Yourself Some Slack	119
57. Liberate Your Inner Child	121

SECTION ELEVEN - Get Rid Of Useless Emotions

58. Forgiveness Is Divine	124
59. Get Rid Of The Guilts	126
60. Look With Courage Into The Face Of Fear	128
61. On Being Judgmental	131
62. Stop Worrying And Start Living	133
63. Stressless Living	134

SECTION TWELVE - You're Very Special

64. It's Okay To Be Different!	138
65. Soar With Your Strengths	140
66. Enjoy The Richness Of Your Personality	142
67. Self Actualization: Your Best You!	144
68. Self Identity	146

SECTION THIRTEEN - Time

69. Gifts Of Time	148
70. Time Management Is Really Self-Management	151
71. Choose Your Day	153
72. Procrastination	155

SECTION FOURTEEN - Your Relationship With Others

73. Seeing Christ In Everyone	157
74. Respect	159
75. Handling Difficult People	161
76. It's The Message Not The Messenger!	163
77. He Has A Good Heart	165
78. Don't Let Another's Opinion Hold You Back	167
79. What Others Teach Us	169

Gratefully . . .

Arthur had Merlin.
I would like to thank my mentors and friends:
George Benson, M.D. & Denis Waitley, Ph.D.

Introduction

What motivates someone to write a book called Simple Psychology?

I contacted the psychology department where I did my graduate work to design a doctorate level program that was neither counseling oriented nor research based. I wanted to study psychological concepts and principles that had simple application value for salespeople. The head of the department said to me, "Tom, you don't understand—this is a research institution. We analyze, theorize, and experiment. What you want to do is very applications oriented. We don't function that way."

I laughed at the irony. I wanted to study everyday problems to develop a psychology of living and achievement that would help people. I read, studied, and thought. Voilà! The beginning of Simple Psychology.

What events in a person's life shape a psychology of living and achievement? Is it education, experience or both? For me, it's the combination of the things I've lived and the things I've studied. I have two degrees in Psychology; lost my father too early; had a troubled adolescence; spent a tour of duty in Vietnam; lost my voice to cancer at age thirty (and now earn a living with it); suffered a total devastation of my office building during the 1993 Midwest floods; and a host of more common distractions along the way.

On the other side of life's balance sheet, I've put myself through college and graduate school; started and operated two successful businesses; have three wonderful children; married to a fantastic woman for 25 years; coached little league baseball and soccer for a decade; successfully served in professional associations; been active in my church; and made strong friendships along the way. All-in-all, it's a wonderful life!

My point is that I find it difficult to separate what I've learned in seven years of formal study of psychology and what I've learned from life along the way. One has taught me the theory of living and the other the practicality of living. No one event prompted this book. It's the synergy of everything I've experienced that appears in these pages. It's a simple psychology of living that may help you cut your learning curve.

When writing a book like this, the author takes several risks. One is that others will consider the work irrelevant. Another is opening oneself to criticism. The third and perhaps most significant risk is to render oneself vulnerable by letting down one's guard and sharing from the heart. I'm willing to take all of these risks if you'll risk reading Simple Psychology. Take a risk by letting it challenge some of your most fundamental beliefs about life. One of two things will happen. You will either become more firm in your convictions, or you will allow yourself to be influenced positively by the thoughts contained in this book.

Read this book on-the-go, at one sitting, and over again. You may find ten pages in this book relevant to your life at this moment. Next year you may find thirty pages relevant. Pass it along to a friend. Learn from it and let it lubricate your mind to develop your own simple psychology of life. At the end of each reading, I

Simple Psychology

summarized with an action tip. These tips are great for daily mental fuel.

This project has been slow. I've been researching and living its contents over forty-five years. It's a book I wrote primarily for me and my children yet feel privileged to share with you. Even though I spent the past three years putting it on paper, I'll spend the rest of my life reading, digesting, and practicing what I've written. I hope you enjoy reading this as much as I've enjoyed writing it.

Happy reading!

Tom Reilly

SECTION ONE

What's Really Important In Life

The readings that appear in this section will challenge some of your fundamental beliefs about what really matters in life. They will bend your comfort zone and make you think! They encourage you to answer the wake-up calls in your life; reflect on the quality of your journey; balance your life; spread a little happiness; open your heart to love; and pray for your children.

1: Wake-Up Call

Life is full of rich experiences that teach us something about our journey through it. I learned one of its lessons during a meeting at which I spoke. The vice president of sales and I were talking before my presentation. One thing led to another, and he mentioned that he liked the anecdotes about my children that I use to illustrate key points.

It was obvious from his comments that he was a family-oriented person. He told me about a family milestone they experienced the week before. The oldest of his six children went away to college for the first time. Because they were such a tight-knit family, the trip in the car was more like a trip down memory lane. "Dad, do you remember when we did this?" "Yeah, and how about the vacation when we went to . . . ?"

The closer they got to the dormitory the more somber the conversation grew. Each family member sensed that this was a major turning point for their family—somehow knowing that their life at home would never be the same with the oldest away at college. They would be a family minus one.

On the trip home, an occasional sniffle broke the silence. Everyone knew this day would come and was excited for the oldest child but now longed for the special family time they shared together. As he related this story with tears in his eyes, my thoughts went to my three children and how my family will deal with this in a few years. We both had lumps in our throats. He told me about the rest of their day. Somehow they muddled through the night.

At precisely 5:30 a.m. the next morning he was awakened by the shrill of an alarm clock piercing the early-morning silence. He reached over to turn it off and realized that it was coming from down the hall. He raced down the hallway hoping to avoid waking the rest of the family. He reached the source of the alarm—the bedroom of his college student. The oldest left the clock with the alarm set. He sat down on the bed and cried silently for a few minutes.

On the way back to his bedroom, he stopped by his youngest child's bedroom, peeked in, smiled at his sleeping little angel, walked over and kissed the child softly on the cheek, sat on the edge of the bed and watched him sleep. He prayed a silent prayer of thanksgiving for this wake-up call. It reminded him that he still had plenty of time to spend with his other children. For him, this was a blessed insight. Rarely, do I walk past the bedrooms of my sleeping children without thinking of his story. And I, too, sit quietly and watch them sleep. Some day my little chicks will fly the coop;

but for now, I'm lucky. My children are young and we have a lot of miles to go before they leave home.

It took a great deal of courage for my friend to share this story with me. This was one of the most private moments in his family's life. I respect this and am indebted to him, for this was my wake-up call, too.

Today I shall answer the wake-up calls I hear and act on them.

2: Success Is The Quality Of Your Journey

Let's play a word association game. What do you think of when you hear the word success? Some respond with the perfunctory, "Money." Others rattle off a shopping list of things they want to acquire. Some even say things like, "Never having to work again."

I doubt there is a single word that evokes a more passionate array of responses than success. For centuries, society's thinkers have spun definitions that reflect the thinkers' values. And today there's still no consensus. Part of the problem is with misconceptions. And regarding success, there are plenty.

First, some people confuse achievement with success. A person who achieves great things in business is called successful. Some individuals may achieve great things in the business world but may fail miserably in their relations with others. Is this person successful? Is success one dimensional? I remember listening to a clergyman on a radio talk show discuss a gentleman who climbed the ladder of corporate success only to discover "it was leaning against the wrong building." I wonder if his family called him a success?

Second, people often confuse the acquisition of things with success. Just ask the child whose parent freely distributes money but is a tightwad when it comes to sharing time with the child. I've seen this in coaching children. Many parents write checks freely but are too committed in other areas to give time. I wonder if these children define success as the ability to give things. Winning is less about scoring and owning as it is giving and being.

Third, success is something to work toward—a goal! What happens when you get there? Do you enjoy the destination or stretch your horizon again in a compulsive drive for more? My own Zen-like discovery hit me one day as I was tooling down the highway atop my motorcycle. I was on a pleasure ride, the wind in my hair with no particular destination; but boy, was I driving fast to get there! I challenged myself, "Isn't the journey the reason for riding this thing?" I rolled back the throttle and enjoyed the ride even more.

If you define success as an end-point to which you aspire, you're <u>not</u> successful until you get there. Conversely, if you define success as the quality of your journey, you become successful with your first step. What if you defined success as living your life in a way that was consistent with your values? Wouldn't success begin the moment you chose and stepped onto this path?

At this moment can you really say, "I'm one of the most successful people I know, not because of what I've acquired, but because of how I'm living the journey and what I've become in the process?"

It may help you clarify your definition of success by writing a success scenario: "For me, success is . . . (and then complete this with your own thoughts)."

For example, it may sound like, "Providing a financially comfortable and loving environment for my family, living a spiritually enhancing lifestyle, achieving independence, working at a meaningful and challenging profession, celebrating friendships, and having fun along the way."

This is a values-driven, goal-achieving lifestyle: a journey of successful living. Write a success scenario that you can begin living today! Then take the first step on your special journey, and in the words of Dr. Suess:

"Congratulations! Today's your day. You're off to great places! You're off and away."

Today I shall focus on the quality of my journey.

3: Balance Your Life

Imagine the business people who have invested a lifetime pursuing a career that with each promotion drew them further away from their families. At the end of their journeys, how many people do you think say, "I wish I would have spent more time at the office"? Few people spend the final days of their lives longing for more time in business.

How many parents, fathers especially, wish they would have given more time to their children? Many successful business people with whom I deal have shared their regrets over spending too much time away from their children.

It's easy to become one dimensional: the workaholic business person; super mom; teacher of the year; a real company man; everyone's grunt; etc. As a one dimensional person, we invest tremendous energy in one area of our lives to the exclusion of others. Imagine how many married couples who, once they begin to have children and become mom and dad, forget that they were once boyfriend and girlfriend, husband and wife.

There's the ubiquitous church worker who gives selflessly to the congregation but forgets there's a family at home. There's the father who leads the community outreach programs while his children desperately need his time at home. What about the volunteer mom who gives all of her time to charitable causes so that her family feels neglected? Is there a therapist reading this book who gives and gives and gives and never receives?

From my own experiences, I've learned that when I give too much attention to my business and neglect my family, I feel guilty for short-changing them. I've also discovered, as a father and husband, that when I give too much time to everyone else's priorities and ignore mine, I begin to resent everyone and everything.

Living one dimensional lives lacks the richness of vast experiences. It deprives you of the beauty of a sunset because you're staring at office walls. You miss the company of good friends because your family demands all your time. You fail your financial obligations because you didn't give this area the proper attention. You've been so busy you haven't had a physical exam in years.

There are seven areas in life to which we must attend if we are to get the most from it: spiritual, family, social, work, health, self interests and financial. Imagine the full life you would lead if every week you attended to each of these seven areas. You could set goals for each area in your life to ensure that you're on track.

Here's a really radical concept. Create an *Ideal Day*. During this day, do something in each of the seven areas of your life. For example, you awaken early in the morning to walk in the early morning sun; you return home to read something that's spiritually enhancing—a visit with your Creator; you have a casual breakfast with your family while discussing everyone's plans for the day; you go to the office and give it your best; have a non-business lunch with a friend; return home that evening for a quiet dinner with your spouse; you review your finances; and spend a few minutes reading the novel you bought six months ago but never got around to reading. Sound unrealistic? Why?

What would your life be like if you lived this way everyday? Financially, you may not earn all the money in the world, but how much richer in living would you be? Food for thought, eh?

Today I shall balance my life: family, spiritual, career, friends, financial, self and community.

4: Less Is More

"You can never get enough of a good thing!" or "Less is more!" Which of these two statements do you believe? Do you go for more or less?

An easy starting point is to determine the things in life we want more of. More money brings security. More health means a quality of life to which everyone aspires. Most spiritual people would consider more spirituality a blessing. More love in your life means a strong sense of belongingness. More friends offer a support network. More talent empowers us to compete vigorously at our profession. More patience makes us easier to be around. More commitment, passion, and enthusiasm give us an edge. More honesty builds trust. More empathy builds understanding. More listening builds relationships. More cooperation builds harmony. More happiness is everyone's pursuit in life.

So why is "more" not a good idea? It may have something to do with those areas in which we pursue more. The other side of the coin is those areas of life in which we should pursue less. Where is less really more?

From my personal experiences, I know that to reduce stress, we must do more of less. We all want less stress: fewer hassles; less pressing deadlines; no ultimatums; and as few anxieties as possible. Less can be more. Would you rather read one great book this month that has great impact on your life or ten mediocre books? Which would you prefer: a single glass of a really good wine, or a gallon of mouthwash? How about an occasional night out at a good restaurant versus frequent visits to the gastronomic hall of shame—fast food places? How about one really meaningful love affair in your life with your spouse, or a string of meaningless one-night stands? As a salesman, am I caught up in the phenomenon called "pipeline-itis"? This is where I'm so obsessed with jamming the front end of my pipeline that I ignore nurturing what I have in place? Am I better off using a few words to communicate a point effectively and succinctly, or become verbose to impress but confuse readers?

Life is a balance sheet. It has two columns: one reads *less* and the other, *more*. How we choose to live our lives fills both columns. Under the *more* column, we begin to acquire and collect things. As we collect them and determine that they're fun but not very meaningful, we fill the *more* column with the intangibles—love, faith, integrity, etc.

Then, the *less* column emerges. We begin to see things more clearly. Age does that to us. Our eyesight may falter but our vision gets better. We want to enjoy fully that which is around us.

On an unconscious level, we determine those things in life we want *more* of, and those things in life we want *less* of, and begin to live to achieve both. A conscious effort of our *more* and *less* lists helps us reach our goals more quickly.

As you complete your list you will discover that you choose to focus on becoming *more* of what you can become and *less* on what you can acquire. You will discover that happiness really comes from your *being* more than your *having* or owning. *Having* is nice and fun. Yet *being* is for the long haul.

Today I shall pursue more of less!

5: Happiness

The elusive state of being. For centuries, great thinkers have written about it. Aristotle concluded that it was the primary thing to which humans aspire. We pursue that which gives us happiness. Everything is incidental to its achievement.

Abraham Lincoln said, "Most people are about as happy as they want to be." Franklin Roosevelt said, "Happiness lies in the joy of achievement, in the thrill of creative effort." William Butler Yeats wrote, "Happiness is neither virtue nor pleasure not this thing nor that but simply growth. We are most happy when we are growing."

In his book, Dennis Wholey said, "No one finds happiness after a long search. It comes to us as the direct result of positive self-worth, specific actions, personal attitudes, and the way in which we relate to other people. Freedom to be ourselves, good feelings, satisfaction, contentment, peace of mind, joy, laughter, and happiness are the rewards of life. They are available to all of us for the doing—not for the wishing, asking, or demanding."

While reading these and many more, two things become crystal clear about that to which all of us aspire. First, if you want to be happy, get busy. It doesn't just happen. We make it happen. It's not passively or randomly distributed among the population. It happens because we make it happen. We are instrumental to our happiness. It has much to do with what we expect and how we pursue these expectations. If you're happy, what are you doing to make yourself happy? If you're unhappy, what's the source of your unhappiness?

Second, happiness is an inner thing, not an external thing. How often do people say things like "I'll be happy when . . ." Fill in the blank: "I graduate from college. We have children. The kids are raised and gone. I retire. I get married. I lose weight. I find a new job. I earn more money. I have more time off. I go to Disneyland." And the list goes on.

When will you be happy?

Happiness comes from the inside out. You can't drink it, snort it, shoot it, eat it, buy it or sell it. But, you can create it. It comes from a sense of satisfaction with oneself. It's a ratio of what you have to give and how fully you give it. It's the answer to the question, "Are you living up to your raw material potential?" Satisfaction comes stretching to the edge of your abilities, and the results are a bonus. It's got a lot more to do with your *being* than your *having*—who you *are*, not what you *own*.

One of our primary needs is self-exploration. We are born curious. We want to discover what's in us. To a degree, happiness has to do with how we pursue this need—how we attempt to satisfy this curiosity. Pearl Buck wrote, "Growth itself contains the germ of happiness."

So, where do we find happiness? Within us and within our reach. It's one-part what we give to ourselves; and since none of us lives in a vacuum, it's one-part what we give to our relationships. We are about as happy as we choose to be.

Today I shall spread a little happiness.

6: Unconditional Love

Love is one of the most studied issues throughout time. The great thinkers have all written about it. Judaism professes, "Thou shalt love thy neighbor as thyself." Buddhism offers, "Full of love for all things in the world, practicing virtue in order to benefit others, this man alone is happy." Jesus commanded, "Love one another even as I have loved you."

What is so magical about this concept that all religions seem to converge on this point? Euripides said, "Love is all we have." "Love is the only gold," said Tennyson.

Loving "unconditionally" is especially important in families. Parents must love their children "as is." To love your children just because they are them is the greatest gift of all.

Imagine your Creator saying to you, "I will love you only if you do certain things." Since no one is perfect, how can we expect to earn the Almighty's love? The good news is we don't have to earn it: it's there—just like the parental love that should be there for the child.

As a parent, I understand how challenging it can be to separate the act from the actor. Our prescription is to separate the two. Never judge a person by their behavior. It adds to the problems.

This is important in other relationships also. How do you think most married people would answer this? "I love you because I need you." Or, "I need you because I love you." Some people accept others "as is." They attach no special conditions to the relationship. "I like you just because you're you." They live in the *acceptance* mode.

Other people operate in an *assessment* mode. They judge and assess before they accept. You earn their attentions. "I like you because you've proven yourself worthy of my affections. You've earned my love." With whom would you rather associate? How would your loved ones describe you? Do you *assess* or do you *accept*?

The assessors promote a cause-and-effect love. "Do this and I will love you." The message is crystal clear. To be loved by me, you must behave in a certain way. Imagine carrying that message around in your head!

Children are wonderful at giving love. It's as natural for them as breathing. Parents punish them, yell at them, abuse them, ground them, limit and inhibit them, and children respond with love.

Unconditional love does not excuse behavior or relieve us from personal responsibility. It's simply, "I love you for you. At times your behavior may be inappropriate and challenge the upper limits of my patience; and still, you're a beautiful person created in the image of your God. I'm very proud to wear the title, Dad. I love you just because you're you."

Just like the lyrics in the Beetles song . . .

"Love is all you need . . ."

Today I shall love unconditionally.

7: Parent's Prayer

The most important job I'll ever have is raising children. The most important title I'll ever wear is "Dad."

Simple Psychology

What I teach my children along the way is the most important lesson plan I'll ever design. I know I must give them a sense of where they come from—their roots. To balance this I must encourage solid independence so they feel comfortable venturing out into the world without mom and dad.

Their ability to make the right choices has a lot to do with what we've taught them along the way. With that in mind, I'd like to share with you a prayer I wrote to remind me of my role in their education. In sharing this with you, I've reminded myself of my role in making these happen. I must first live them at home. Children are very attuned to our walking our talk. They're fantastic observers and remember most of what they hear and see.

"Lord help my children make right choices in life. Help them choose . . .

"Love not hate; right not wrong; frugality not waste; prudence not promiscuity; integrity not deceit; concern not indifference; sharing not hoarding; respect not contempt; understanding not judging; pride not arrogance; humility not vanity; patience not impulsiveness; conviction not vacillation; growth not stagnation; perseverance not quitting; to leave a little bigger wood pile than the one they found when they came into this world; and to follow the path to You!"

Today I shall pray with and for my children.

SECTION TWO

The World Is A Big Sand Box

How big is your world? Each of us is a small part of something much bigger than ourselves, and we need to be reminded of this periodically. The readings in this section encourage you to give back something to society; look for ways to make a difference in this world; leave a little bigger woodpile than the one you found; and to recognize the value of "We."

8: Life Is Bigger Than Me

One of our earliest childhood realities is that life is bigger than us. We are part of something greater than a society of one. Therefore, we must give back part of ourselves to the thing of which we're a part.

It's absurd that we can live in a world, a country, a state, a community, or a family, and not give back something from our gain. Isn't it true that plants draw from the soil and the sun and give back to the air we breathe? The crops that farmers plant take from the sun, the soil, and the rain, and nourish the inhabitants of the earth. The harmony and balance of nature is built around this fundamental dynamic of give and take. This explains why some of the happiest people I know are those who give back so much of what life has given them.

Some of the most miserable people I know are so preoccupied with themselves that they fail to see the bigger world of which they are a part. They are stuck in the "me-me-me" mode.

Few things are as boorish as watching "a very important man in his own mind" muddle his way through life. It's as if the world should spin on his axis.

Why do some people give tirelessly and others covet gratuitously? One possibility is that the taker was neither taught that he was part of something bigger than himself, nor allowed to feel a part of it.

How unfortunate for society when we do not fully utilize the skills and talents that each of us possesses.

Throughout history from philosophers to politicians and singers to writers, people have recognized the importance and obligation of humans to give back something to a world of which they are a small but integral part. It's our philosophical legacy for generations to follow. William Danforth wrote:

"Our most valuable possessions are those which can be shared without lessening: they are those which, when shared, multiply. Our least valuable possessions are those which, when divided, are diminished."

Could it be that the more we give of ourselves, the more we discover about ourselves?

Today I shall give back to the society of which I'm a part.

9: Can I Make A Difference?

This question haunts many of us. It bespeaks our insecurity for leaving a positive mark on this earth—our contribution to the greater good of humanity—our defining effort at immortality. If I try, can I really make a difference?

Several years ago while I was listening to Denis Waitley's cassette series, <u>Seeds of Greatness</u>, he introduced me to Loren Eiseley's work. Eiseley was a humanist, naturalist, educator, and anthropologist. Some have anointed him the twenty-first century Thoreau. He wrote prolifically on man's place in the world. His essay, <u>The Star Thrower</u>, metaphorically describes our ability to make a difference in this world. I've read this piece at least six times—each time finding greater meaning and depth than the last. I will probably read it six more times before I fully appreciate its depth.

In <u>The Star Thrower</u>, Eiseley describes his experiences on the beaches of Costabel. Walking along the moonlit beach one night, he was astonished by the sight of the debris of life littering the beaches: starfish blanketed the area—some dead, others clinging desperately to life. To paraphrase Eiseley, the sea had cast aside its offspring. Walking further, he discerned a lone figure dancing ceremoniously in the shadows of the moonlight: bending, kneeling, reaching, and throwing.

As Eiseley approached, the stranger knelt again, picked up something and threw it beyond the breaking waves. "It may live," said the thrower, "if the offshore pull is strong enough . . . the stars throw well. One can help them."

Eiseley scanned the thousands of starfish and the

challenge overwhelmed him—too many starfish and too few star throwers. He was torn between his cynicism and his admiration for the star thrower. He wrestled with this for some time and in the end understood the message of the star thrower. One makes a difference where one can. He returned several days later and became a star thrower, too.

The star thrower expected nothing in return. He threw to make a difference. It was an act of great compassion—selfless giving. This is true servitude. And every star he threw boomeranged with something for him: life.

I've known star throwers. They move silently through life, doing what they can, when they can, for whomever they can. They are the guardians of our civilization: the Mother Teresa's, the nurses, the teachers and preachers and even the lowliest of God's creatures. Just as Eiseley's Star Thrower gave life, these modern day star throwers give life to the debris our world casts aside.

Each day as we walk along our own personal Costabel beach, past the debris life has strewn about, and we must decide. Will we kneel down, collect a starfish, and throw it beyond the breaking waves? Or, will we simply move on, ignoring the opportunity? I believe that you will carefully pick up the starfish, and with great compassion, hurl it back to life. For in you, too, is a star thrower.

Today I shall become a star thrower.

Simple Psychology

10: Can I *Really* Make A Difference?

In the previous reading, I introduced <u>The Star Thrower</u>. Every day we meet star throwers in every walk of life: police officers who could have chosen a safer job; teachers who are underpaid for the work they do; and the armies of volunteers who operate charitable organizations. Some star throwers are highly visible. Most lead lives of quiet inspiration.

I met a star thrower in a seminar one day. He approached me during break and said, "Tom, you know all that stuff you talk about—being customer driven. I really believe in it. I used to be in sales for my company. Now, I'm in purchasing.

"When I was in sales, a woman visited our store one day and inquired about a software program for learning disabled children. I confirmed we had it. She asked if I would spend time with her learning-disabled son when she returned. I agreed, thinking it was the common small talk between buyer and seller.

"On the following weekend, the Saturday before Christmas, one of the busiest shopping days of the year, she returned with her son, in a wheelchair. He was a paraplegic and learning-disabled. I made good on my promise and spent the next hour with him at the computer terminal.

"While I demonstrated this software package I could see from the corner of my eye the six-deep line of people at the counter. I was a commissioned salesman missing one of the best selling opportunities of the year. Any box passing over the counter that day would have been extra income for me. I had mixed feelings. On the one hand, I felt good because I was in the giving mode.

23

On the other hand, I felt disappointed because I was missing income opportunities. That turned out to be an emotional tug of war I felt all weekend.

"I finished the software demonstration within an hour, and the wave of customers had come and gone. I sold the hundred-dollar package and missed one of the biggest money-making opportunities of the season. Such is the life of a salesperson. But, I still felt good about helping this little guy.

"I thought about this a few more times throughout the weekend. I was proud of myself yet disappointed with the missed income opportunities.

"On Tuesday a gentleman visited our store and asked for me by name.

He said, "Are you the salesman who helped a woman and learning-disabled boy last weekend?"

"Yes, sir. I am."

"That was my wife and he was my son. I wanted to come in here and thank you personally. As you could see, the little guy doesn't have a lot to feel good about; but, when he came home Saturday, he was on fire with enthusiasm because of the time you spent with him and the software we purchased. If you've ever wondered, 'Have I made a difference in this world?' you made a difference in our world this week. I had to thank you personally for this.

"By the way, my company needs eight personal computers, and I'd like you to have the order!"

The former salesman smiled at me and turned away. As he did, I recalled Eiseley's Star Thrower and knew I just met one. That December, a young salesman became a star thrower. He knelt down, picked up a starfish and gently threw it back to the sea—giving it life. Did he make a difference? For that one he did. The follow-up sale was incidental: a bonus. He neither expected nor solicited it. It came to him—the starfish returning the favor.

So, we return to the question, "Can I really make a difference?" Unequivocally, the answer is, "Yes, for at least one starfish, you can."

Today I shall make a difference in someone's life.

11: Leave A Little Bigger Woodpile Than The One You Found!

The givers in this world impress me. They seem to have endless time and energy for others. They're always there. The same people time and again. And they're always smiling! For givers, the act of giving appears to be the closest thing to perpetual energy. They draw energy from giving energy. This is the boomerang effect in life: you get back that which you throw out. Thackeray stated it more eloquently when he said, "Life is like a mirror. You get back what you put into it." Others have said, "It's more blessed to give than to receive."

Givers give selflessly. They expect nothing in return. They are more concerned about leaving a bigger woodpile than the one they found when they entered this world. They may not save the world, but they make a difference where they can.

Then, there are the takers. They believe that their

lot in life entitles them to take whatever they can get, whenever they can get it, and from whomever they can get it. Their hands are always out. It's as if their umbilical chords are hanging out looking for another womb to plug into.

In sales, it's the salesperson who will encourage the customer to buy, regardless of needs. In business, it's the manager who demands everything from employees but never reciprocates with appreciation or recognition. In life, it's the person who asks, and asks, and takes—never giving in return. It's the parent who enrolls his child in everything but rarely helps out.

Givers focus on the difference they can make, however small. It's a simple philosophy to live by, "Am I in the giving mode or the taking mode?"

At times you may find yourself in a situation where you need the help—the receiving end for a while. May you have the humility to accept help when the time comes. It's not easy for givers to accept help. After all, they're accustomed to giving.

If we give as freely as our situation permits and receive as graciously as we give, we will strike a balance in life. When you meet a giver, the focus is always on you. They are concerned about your welfare. The conversation focuses on your issues. And, the giver just won't stop listening!

I wonder if they have discovered the basic truth in life that if I concern myself with your problems, mine may seem small by comparison.

Today I shall leave a little bigger woodpile than the one I found.

12: We Is Greater Than Me

"No man is an island." Generations have passed this wisdom down from one to another. Perhaps, now more than any time in history, we depend on each other. The city dweller depends on the farmer for food. The farmer feeds off the wages of the city dweller. We drive autos built by someone else, repaired by someone else and fueled by someone else. Something in our house breaks and we call a handy man to fix it.

The renaissance man—the pinnacle of independence and self-reliance—exists more in lore than life today. We all depend on each other for something. I learned this the hard way fighting a battle with cancer.

When I think back to what made a difference in my life, it was my support group. I awakened in the intensive care unit to my wife's tearful explanation of how sick I was. She immediately added, "Someone in the pharmacy got a prayer line going for you at their church." I can remember the tear running down my cheek. Almost overnight, a close-knit group of people stepped into my life, and I felt their love.

A priest, who became a good friend, provided us with the spiritual help we needed. He inspired me with the words of St. Ignatius Loyola, "Pray as if it all depends on God and work as if it all depends on you." He encouraged me to be active in my prayerful requests. He admonished: "Pray, trust, and do."

My doctor was crucial. He saved my life. And he did it with the bedside manner of a special friend. He was always there. He knew when to use humor and when to be serious. He always spoke the truth, even when it wasn't what I wanted to hear.

My sister, Elizabeth, was our beacon as things got a little foggy. When I was younger, she was my surrogate mother because my real mother was in the hospital for months. She was playing that special role again. Nurturing. Hoping. Praying. Laughing. Helping and hugging us. We could not have done it without her. Thanks, Liz!

And then there was Jennifer, my speech therapist. What can I say about someone who spent three days a week for six months helping me recover my voice. She saw my anger, frustration, depression, and joy. And she was always there, too.

We had a prayer group to which we belonged. We met every Wednesday evening at our country church. During these prayer sessions, our friends included us in their prayers. Outside of these meetings, they called us to check on how we were doing. Always there: loving, praying, and supporting.

The sages were right, none of us is an island. No one can nor should have to do it alone. It takes a special person to give this kind of support. It requires a strong measure of humility to receive it. I learned well. We is greater than me.

And my spiritual experience has taught me an even more important lesson in life. If we is greater than me, then He is greater than me or we!

Today I shall give back to the team of which I'm a member.

SECTION THREE

Positive Attitude

At a gut level, everyone understands attitude. We all recognize a good one and can smell a bad one a mile away. These readings illustrate how to control your attitude; program yourself for success; convert your beliefs into behavior; and look for the blessings in your burdens.

13: Making Lemonade

Everyone's heard the old saying, "When you get lemons, make lemonade." It's easy to say, but hard to do. This spotlights one of the fundamental principles of applied psychology: how to process life. It's your way of perceiving and reacting to what life hands you. Some choose to view things positively while others view things negatively.

Are there people who enjoy being miserable? Do some people love to hate? Are there others who prefer pessimism? The answer is a qualified, "Yes." No one is born cynical. In fact, life itself is the physical expression of spiritual optimism. To say one is born negative is like saying we all are born to be sick—not true. Cynicism, negativism, and skepticism are learned.

Therapists work with people to help shape their perceptions of the world. Perceptual distortions are a major cause of ineffective coping strategies. Cognitive restructuring or reframing helps the person view life from more than one perspective.

I was sitting at our breakfast table drinking coffee watching our little guy, Paul, play in the yard with his broken Big Wheel—the oversized low-riding tricycle. His was broken at the neck so that all that remained was the plastic handlebars attached to the big front wheel. I went out to talk with him.

"What's up, Paul?" I asked.

"Nothing, Dad. Just playing," he said.

"Well, I can see that. You know, Paul, we could go down to the toy store this afternoon and get a new Big Wheel," I said.

"Don't worry about it, Dad. My birthday's next month. I can wait."

"Are you sure, son?"

"Sure Dad, I'm fine. I've got my one wheeler."

"What do you mean, one wheeler?" I asked.

"My one wheeler. This thing. I can go anywhere with it. I can take it up and down the hill, around the bushes, in and out of the sandbox, and besides, Dad, I'm the only one in the neighborhood with a one wheeler!"

I gulped real hard, nodded and walked slowly to the house. Out of the mouth of a babe came ageless optimism. I saw a broken toy. He saw a unique toy. The event was the same, but our perceptions were different. For years, I kept the one wheeler in the corner of our garage as a constant reminder of how to frame life . . . optimistically. It's always my choice how I want to process life.

Today I shall make lemonade when the world hands me a lemon.

Simple Psychology

14: Positive Mental Programming

Mental programming is how you talk to yourself—the software that runs your mental program. It results in positive behavior, or a "systems-error" message.

How you talk to yourself follows the G.I.G.O. principle: garbage in—garbage out; good in—good out. These programming tips will help you write positive code messages to replay over and again.

Focus on what you want versus what you don't want. If you focus on what you want to avoid, you are concentrating on negative consequences. It's difficult to perform well when you're focusing on the thing you don't want to happen. In baseball we teach players to step into the pitch, not "Don't step out." Before a big speech you're better off repeating positive affirmations of how well you'll perform, not "Don't blow this one." Standing on the first tee on a golf course, it's easy to say to yourself, "Don't slice. You've got a lot of folks watching." A more positive mental image is to visualize your well-executed swing and the desired end result.

Concentrate on what you want to happen and how you will create it. Focus on the thing over which you have the most control—your effort. You may not be able to control the outcome of your efforts, but you can control what you put into it.

If you're dreaming about earning a living as a musician but only work at it part-time now while driving a lift truck, change your mental picture. See yourself as a musician who is working temporarily as a lift truck operator.

Reframe when your mental alarm sounds. Program your mental alarm to sound when you think negatively. Step back and ask, "Is there a more positive way to view this?" There generally is. Use positive choice. Your ability to view things from different positions encourages positive responses.

Light your fuse with dreams. Dream big dreams. Let your mind travel across continents and galaxies. Imagine what it would be like if you achieved these dreams. Dreams give hope and fuel your journey with enthusiasm. Few things will lift your spirits as dreaming big dreams. Take a mental journey to the land of your dreams and feel the passion. You dreamt a lot as a child. Big dreams occupied your vast imagination. You can use that same power to program yourself to achieve great things by dreaming of them and replaying the image daily.

Pat yourself on the back. Enjoy how far you've come. Concentrate on how well you've performed, not the mistakes you've made. You will make a lot of mistakes. We all do. It's okay. That's one of your inalienable rights as a human being—to make lots of mistakes on your journey.

When you're at the crossroads of success and failure remember the right things you've done, not the wrong ones. It's like the baseball pitcher who has thrown several strikeouts in a game, has two down in the present inning, but is preoccupied with the last few walks he gave up. Give yourself a break.

Positive mental programming is how you want a loved one to speak to himself or herself. Be kind to yourself, for you, too, are a loved one.

Today I shall program myself for success.

15: Believe And Behave

Attitude drives behavior and behavior changes attitude. Sounds like double talk, doesn't it? And yet there's truth in both. If you want to change your behavior, work on your attitude. If you want to change your attitude, work on your behavior. I call this the attitude—behavior reciprocity.

Our work with organizations has taught us that if the attitude is in place, the behavior naturally follows. If people want to serve, they behave in ways to serve others better. Whether it's a church group, children's athletic team, or business, people behave in ways to support their attitudes. Attitudes drive behavior.

Earl Nightingale's greatest discovery was the six words that changed his life: "We become what we think about." This was the predecessor of creative visualization. If we believe that we can behave in a certain way, we will likely act this out. Our beliefs and attitudes not only affect our behavior—they drive it. It's cause and effect. If we want to change behavior, start with what we believe or think about.

A few years ago I purchased a Stearman biplane, a W.W. II open-cockpit trainer. I flew it from New Hampshire to St. Louis. It was fantastic! On the trip, my co-pilot yelled through the intercom, "Are you looking out the left side of the plane?"

"Yeah," I responded.

A few minutes passed and he yelled, "Are you looking out the right side of the plane?" Again, I confirmed his suspicion.

The third time he asked in which direction I was looking I responded, "Why do you ask?"

Simple Psychology

He said, "Wherever you look, the wings of the plane dip in that direction." He was referring to the automatic behavioral response of my hand on the stick. If I looked to the right, my hand unconsciously moved the stick right and the plane followed. If I looked left, I unconsciously pointed the stick left. The plane followed. Unless I corrected for this, it flew my line of sight.

Like the Stearman, we travel in the direction of our thoughts. If we preoccupy ourselves with the message that we're inferior to another, we may end up by making ourselves inferior in some fashion. If we foster beliefs that we cannot do something, we may result in being incapable of doing this thing. We behave as we believe.

As a salesperson, if I approach a customer with negative expectations of the outcome, I shall surely fail. If I believe myself to be successful and behave accordingly, I shall prevail more than fail.

So how do I change my beliefs? It reminds me of the old prayer, "Lord, it's not my faith that's the problem. Help my disbelief." Since belief drives behavior, the principle of reciprocity mandates that behavior drives belief. It admonishes, "Behave until you believe."

Research demonstrates that if there's a gap between your attitude and your behavior, the attitude will shift to fit your behavior rather than the other way around. If you want to change your attitude, change your behavior. Behave until you believe. And then let your beliefs drive future behavior.

In the speaking profession, there's a popular saying, "Fake it till you make it." This is the same philosophy. Another way of saying this is "Act new until it becomes you." or "Do, and it becomes you." If you want to believe a certain way, behave in a certain way.

If you want to live life more positively, change your thinking and perceptions. The quickest way to change your thinking is to change your behavior. We become that which we think about and think about that which we become.

Life is full of opportunities to choose the positive over the negative. It starts with our beliefs and behaviors. You can choose to believe and behave in a certain way. What's your choice?

Today I shall change my beliefs with positive behavior.

16: Burdens And Blessings

Be careful what you ask for in this life—you may get it! Sound advice or blind caution? Many things we experience in life come packaged either as a blessing or a burden. There are gray areas of course, but most people will perceive something as a blessing or a burden.

In reality, whatever comes your way may have elements of both. Earning a lot of money exacts a price. You must painstakingly manage it. You may even need to employ investment counselors. The price of stardom is a lack of privacy. Everywhere you go people shake your hand and want your autograph. Living in a big beautiful house requires tireless maintenance.

On the other side of the ledger are what appear to be burdens. Losing a job forces many people into careers they might not otherwise consider. Falling ill to a disease encourages some to value every sunset. Financial ruin may cause another to re-evaluate the most important things in life. A friend of mine, who is a professional speaker, told me how he finished a speech for which four hundred people gave him a hearty standing ovation. He went home after this wonderful experience and his wife asked him to take out the trash. I said, "That must have been quite a contrast for you."

He smiled and said, "Yes, my wife has made it her personal mission to help me keep my feet planted firmly on the ground." A burden to go with his blessing!

What's the point? When a burden comes your way, there may be some greater good that will come from it. Is there only pain in every burden we face? I believe there is only pain if that's all we anticipate and look for. The good may not equal the pain, but on which would you rather focus?

The other side of the coin is that when you pursue a blessing, be aware of the sacrifices along the way. We all make trade-offs in this world. It's crucial to manage them in a way that suits your values and long-term goals.

I commented to a friend who works from his home how I missed the days when my speaking business was simple enough to operate from my home. It's been thirteen years since I've run my business from my house. Since then, I have purchased an office building as my training center. It's a true blessing in terms of service to clients.

A month after lamenting to my friend, the Great Flood of '93 hit St. Louis. We took eleven feet of water in our building: the burden. During recovery, I got my wish. We worked out of my house for four months. We had three secretarial desks in our living room. Our dining room was the shipping room. And our three-car garage became the warehouse.

And yet in that devastation, there was an opportunity for us to rebuild our training center with the improvements that I had been considering for a while. It wasn't painless, but we chose to focus on the blessing that emerged from the burden. It also confirmed something else I rediscovered along the path: be careful for what you wish, you may get it!

Today I shall pursue the blessings in my burdens.

17: Adversity Brings Out The Best In You

"I feel like a summa cum laude graduate of the University of Adversity with a Ph.D. in survival" reflects the ex-cancer patient. Show me someone who has achieved something in life, and I'll show you someone who has triumphed over adversity. Volumes are written about the underdog who had to overcome significant obstacles to win.

I was sitting in church one Sunday listening to an inspiring sermon on adversity. I thought there was some pretty good stuff in there I might be able to use in a seminar one day. Later that afternoon, I went to the airport where I kept my Stearman biplane. I planned to go for a relaxing Sunday flight around St. Louis. As I pulled my plane from the hanger, I heard an ominous thud from the runway. It sounded like a dumpster lid slamming shut—a friend of mine flew his airplane into the ground. Before we could get to the wreckage, his plane was totally engulfed in flames. He died on impact.

I hangered my plane and went home. I sat with my wife and told her what happened. Obviously, I was saddened and shook. As we sat in silence I believe we came to the same conclusion at about the same time. At times like this, each of us must reach deep inside ourselves to find that special pocket of strength we didn't know existed before the crisis. We didn't know we had it because we didn't need it until the crisis.

It's a special kind of energy that gives us just enough strength to get up the next morning, take a few deep breaths, lick our wounds, and get through the day. And then we do the same thing all over again the next day—each day using this bit of strength to make it through that day. Day after day we go on living, dipping into this reservoir and drawing enough strength to get by.

Then a transition phase sets in and we begin to feel that we'll make it after all. Today hurts but it's a little better than yesterday. And tomorrow hurts, but it's a hair better than today. If we allow this special strength to do its job, we grow as we emerge from the adversity. What happens to this pocket of energy once the brunt of the adversity passes?

It's still there! It's on-call any time we need it. This is the special secret that people who experience adversity discover: they're stronger than they know. They may not feel it at the time, but the strength is there.

And for those who accept this, they are changed forever by the experience. They grow even stronger.

They develop a tough-minded resilience that won't let them quit. Adversity brings out their personal best. The power they used to survive they now use to thrive. You see it in their eyes. It's a deeply-felt resolve to persist and triumph.

This is the conclusion my wife and I reached the gloomy Sunday afternoon Ray died. Was it easy? No. Was I anxious about flying my plane again after witnessing a fatal accident? Yes. Was this a tough way to learn about resilience and adversity? You bet it was. It was tough for all of us who liked Ray and called him our friend. And I'm sure it was and is a lot tougher on the two-year-old son he left behind.

Perhaps this little guy will consider himself a graduate of the University of Adversity. My guess is he'll make it and then some! He comes from good stock. He'll find that little pocket of strength, latch on to it, and emerge a tougher, more compassionate person.

Today I shall persist victoriously.

18: It's Not So Much What Happens To You . . .

Life is ". . . ninety percent of what I put into it and only ten percent of what it hands me," said the ex-gang member who now works with other gang members encouraging them to take a different path in life. His message is refreshingly straightforward, "It's not so much what happens to us in life but what we do about it that counts."

Most of us spend too much time worrying about the things over which we have little or no control. We live better when we invest our mental energy in those areas where we have control.

This simple formula describes how we process the events in our world and our reactions to them:

EVENT + PERCEPTION = REACTION

We control two of the variables in this formula: our perception of an event and our reaction to the perception. If we control our perception, we control our reaction. Shaping our reactions comes from reshaping our perceptions.

Cognitive restructuring (reframing) is one of the fastest-growing areas in applied psychology. People can perceive things in different ways. Consequently, they are not locked into automatic and rigid thinking patterns.

It offers room for individual application. Start by challenging your initial perceptions of a situation. For example, let's suppose you are not invited to a golf outing with upper management. One perception is that since you did not grow up around the club scene you wouldn't fit in, and they didn't want you to feel out of place. Another perception is that your last report wasn't good enough, and this is management's way of spanking you. Another possibility is that there is a downsizing in the future, and you're sure that your name is on the hit list. How do you feel after considering these possibilities? Pretty miserable I bet.

Is there another way to view this? Sure there is. Maybe you're not a golfer. Perhaps this is a group of managers who started the company and every year have an "original four" golf outing. They could be meeting to discuss an outside business venture they want to pursue. Now how do you feel? The event is the same; but the perception is different, and your reaction changes. The event did not change. You did—by the way you perceived the event. Your perception led you to interpret the event differently. This determines your reaction.

Ask yourself, "Is there another way to explain what's happening?" It's testing your assumptions about reality. For those people caught in the victim mindset, there is only one way to perceive life—through the eyes of a victim. They rarely look for other legitimate reasons why things failed to work out for them. Unfortunately, they may not discover what it takes to lift themselves from victim status. What they don't know holds great inhibiting power over them.

Remember, it's not so much the event that determines your reaction, it's how you choose to view it. Is there another way you can perceive the event? Try this simple reframing exercise and see how it affects your reaction.

Give yourself the benefit of a couple of different perspectives. It will change the way you view your world and, more importantly, how you choose to respond to the events around you.

Today I shall reframe my perception of events that trouble me.

SECTION FOUR

Focused Effort

Focus plays a major role in everyone's life. It's difficult to imagine that anything significant is ever achieved without it. These readings encourage you to focus your energies with laser-like intensity; make strong commitments; be patiently persistent; take pride in and pursue excellence in all you do.

19: Focusing

Focusing is concentrating your efforts with laser-beam intensity on the high-priority activities that help you achieve your goals. If you maintain your focus, avoid distractions along the way, and concentrate your energy on this priority, you'll write an amazing success story.

The late, great Earl Nightingale wrote of the Law of Sacrificed Alternatives. Anytime you choose to do something, you automatically eliminate other things you could do at that moment. As you read a book, you eliminate all other books you could read at that time. When you choose a certain restaurant, you eliminate all other places you could be at that moment.

He articulated an urgency for people to invest time prudently. The message is clear: your actions move you closer to or farther from your goals.

Focusing involves four key elements. First, it begins with a vision or mission. This direction or sense of purpose is your life track. It's where you're headed. Goals support this mission. As your vision becomes clearer, your goals are more focused. Until you're clear on your direction, goals mean little.

Second, once your vision is clear and your goals support this mission, you must have a plan to pursue them. This is your strategy and tactics. The strategy is *what* you plan to do and the tactics are *how* you plan to do it.

Third, you must be willing to make the resource investment: time, money, and effort. Will you allocate the time you need to make your goals happen? Will you make the financial investment even if it's painful? Are you willing to pay the price?

Fourth, discipline of effort. This is your stick-to-itiveness. In plain terms, do you have the guts to remain focused, stick to your plan, and pursue your goals? You must resist the temptations along the path. They're always there. *Lock in* on your mission and *lock out* the noise that distracts you. If your focus is clear, your goals reasonable, and your plan sound, the discipline of effort is easier.

If you have a good plan, reasonable goals, a clear vision, and have invested in its pursuit and struggle with distractions, try positive procrastination.

Positive procrastination is putting off until tomorrow that which distracts us today. For example, if you want to quit something, delay quitting until tomorrow. If you want to blow your diet, wait until tomorrow to eat that candy bar. If you decide to throw in the towel on the novel you've been writing, do it after you finish the next chapter?

We often quit too early. If we hang in there a bit

longer, we can work through the tough times and distractions.

So, are you focused? Are you a maniac on a mission? Do your goals support your vision? Will you make the investment of time, energy, and money? Are you willing to *lock in* on your goal and *lock out* the distractions?

Show me someone who walks with purpose on a worthwhile path in life; who willingly makes the necessary sacrifices; never loses sight of the vision, and I'll show you someone who is truly focused.

Today I shall focus with laser-beam intensity on the opportunities I want to pursue.

20: Make A Commitment To Commit

We're big on commitments in our house. There are days when our children rue the day I learned the word. To commit is to pledge or promise to do something. It has strength and permanence.

Sometimes our children would rather do almost anything other than go to music or dance lessons. There are times they would rather hang out with friends than go to sports practice. I intercede, and they honor their commitments. Having coached for a number of years, I have first-hand experience of what happens when team members ignore their commitments to practice and play hard.

Commitment describes your sincerity and the effort you'll expend. If you commit to something and fail to deliver, what does that really say about your commitment from the start?

Commitment is a way of examining whether you're totally immersed in what you do. You never discover your potential at something unless you totally immerse yourself in its pursuit. H. G. Wells wrote:

"Wealth, notoriety, place, and power are no measures of success whatever. The only true measure of success is the ratio between what we might have done and been on the one hand, and the thing we have made and the thing we have made of ourselves on the other."

One measure of your commitment is the extent to which you will inconvenience yourself. Will you ignore the distractions along the way? Will you sacrifice for your commitment? Will you persevere to make it happen?

How much you're willing to put into something is a strong indicator of the commitment you should make. If you won't give it the time and effort, save others the frustration and yourself the embarrassment of not delivering on your commitments.

I'm concerned that if I teach my children it's okay to relax on their commitments, they'll amble through life always falling a bit short of discovering their potential. They may require a gentle nudge to get started, and plenty of encouragement along the way.

As a manager, if I ignore my commitments how can I reasonably expect my employees to live up to their commitments? As a coach, if I give marginal commitment to the team, how can I expect their full effort? And If I don't honor my commitments as a father and husband, what type of role model am I for my children?

It's not always easy living up to commitments or walking the talk. Sometimes it's downright tough.

That's where the old saying about the tough getting going comes into play. That's something to consider before taking the plunge. But for now, live what you promised. You'll feel better about it. I promise.

"Wheresoever you go, employ all your heart."

(Confucius)

Today I shall commit selectively and live these commitments wholeheartedly.

21: Delayed Gratification: Patient Persistence

The knowing is easy but the doing is tough. Like discipline and patience, delayed gratification makes sense, but it's difficult to implement. We begin life as instant-gratification seekers. We are hungry and want the bottle now. We fill our diapers and want them changed. We see a toy and demand it immediately.

Somewhere along the way, we learn to quell our impulses in favor of long-term gain. This is delayed gratification. Whether it's studying for a test; training for a sporting event; or dieting, delaying gratification is necessary to achieve any measure of success. It's patient persistence.

Discipline, commitment, self-control, stick-to-itiveness require surrendering oneself to a goal. Patient persistence, steadiness, and perseverance are inner gyros that guide us through distractions and temptations along the way. We need to lock in on a course of action and lock out the noise we experience in the process of achieving our goal.

We teeter between impatience, sometimes called sense of urgency or enthusiasm, and our willingness to delay the immediate gain for the long-term, full-scale benefit.

Patient persistence begins with a clear understanding of the end result and the long-term gain. What's your goal? Why do you want it? What's the outcome of your achieving it? How does achieving it overshadow short-term gratification? Will succumbing to the temptation build a better life for you in the long-run? If you quit, how much ground will you need to make up? What will a break in the momentum really mean to you?

Reinforce yourself along the way. Plan for interim rewards that support your efforts. In the short term, you can run on the passion or enthusiasm for a new adventure. For the long haul, you need a system in place. Reward yourself during those tough moments. There are times when defying the urge to quit is good enough. Remind yourself of what you want to accomplish and why it's important to you. If you feel like quitting, remember that you can quit tomorrow when you're thinking clearer.

Renew your passion with symbols of your goal. If you're working diligently to win an incentive trip to Hawaii, get a travel brochure and paste it to your bulletin board. Buy a lei and wear it. Go shopping for your vacation clothes. Carry a Hawaiian resort brochure with a picture of the emerald green waters to reinforce your commitment. Review these, especially when you feel the temptation to quit.

Fuel your desire along the way. It's no different than fueling your car for a long journey. You can't get there on a single tank of gas. You need to refuel often. A single reminder of your goal is insufficient. Surround yourself with the message.

If you fail, remember that you're human: it happens. You're not the first person to stumble along the path. Everyone does. Stay the course. Get back on schedule. You've experienced only a detour—not the end of the journey.

Today I shall persist patiently.

22: Perfection Versus Excellence

Consider the difference between someone who pursues excellence in what he does and another who works toward perfection. One is a healthy philosophy of living. The other is a neurotic drive to achieve an improbable standard. Even the word, *perfection*, paints an image of an uptight efficiency expert attempting to shave micro seconds off a task.

Excellence stimulates a different image: an individual pursuing the best one has to offer. Excel comes from the Latin word, *excelerre*, which means to "surpass or to rise from." It's rising above what one normally does in the course of human activity. It's going beyond everyday standards.

Perfection is defined as "to make or do without flaws, defects, and omissions; completely correct, accurate, and precise." A flawless performance is a measure of excellence. Zero defects is a measure of one's commitment to excellence in production. Perfection is the natural by-product of a commitment to excellence in everything we do.

Your focus must be on that over which you have the most control: your effort. When you meet someone who is truly committed to a personal standard of excellence, the quality of their efforts is the envy of their peers and an industry benchmark. Conversely, if you meet someone who is obsessed with perfection, you see a frustrated, haggard individual pursuing superhuman standards.

Committing to excellence is a lifestyle choice: "I give it my best each and every time I step up to the plate." Being a perfectionist means doing everything flawlessly regardless of your abilities and the conditions at the time. Nothing less than perfect is acceptable. How many people can live their lives committed to that standard?

One can commit to performing with a sense of excellence. I may not be the perfect father, but I'm giving it my best. I may not be the perfect husband, yet I'm committed to excellence in my efforts. I may not be a perfect golfer, but I excel at my attempts. No one can demean the efforts or results of those who are committed to excellence in what they do.

Excellence is giving it your best with available resources. It's the pride you feel that comes from your tireless effort and commitment to the mission. "We've given our best and become our best. We left no stone unturned in the pursuit of excellence." This is the theme of those committed to excellence.

For those committed to excellence, they live by the question, "Is this the best I can do?" Those committed to perfection ask, "Is it perfect yet?"

In most cases, perfection is an elusive, frustrating,

and unrealistic standard. Excellence is a simple psychology in which everyone can participate.

Today I shall pursue excellence in all that I do.

23: P.R.I.D.E.

For two of the four years I served in the U. S. Army, I was a Drill Sergeant. Completing Drill Sergeant school was one of the toughest things I've done—both mentally and physically. It lasted seven weeks, and I wanted to quit every day.

At the time, my wife and I lived off-post in a mobile home. My day started at 4:00 a.m., I would rise, shower, eat a quick breakfast, and be at school by 5:00 a.m. for physical training, PT, or as we called it: physical torture.

We attended class all day; stood rigorous inspections; studied leadership, weaponry, and training methods; drilled in formation; and had plenty of homework for the evening. What was the reward for this grueling pace? The coveted Drill Sergeant badge, whistle, and the Smoky-The-Bear hat. Notwithstanding the extra $75.00 pay per month, was it worth it? You bet! The pride and satisfaction of achievement was something I could wear the rest of my life.

One thing I remember clearly from this school was a poster displaying the acronym, P-R-I-D-E:

Professional Results In Daily Effort

It was positive mental programming. I stared at it daily for seven weeks and absorbed the simple message that professional results come from daily effort. Not from accidental, sporadic, or casual effort but daily effort. It's the persistent expenditure of positive energy toward a worthy goal that yields professional results.

They drilled into our heads that professionalism was more of a state-of-mind, an attitude, and not an income. It resulted from serious and concentrated study of our profession.

Today, a quarter of a century later, the message is just as relevant. It's aged well. My experiences have validated that P.R.I.D.E. is a simple philosophy: daily effort, daily commitment, daily investment of oneself. All of these yield professional results.

So, the focus turns to you. Will you embrace the message? You're a volunteer. No one has forced you to work at your profession. Do you take pride in what you do? Are you a professional? Are you getting professional results? Are you giving it daily effort? Take pride in what you do. It's a simple prescription for success.

Martin Luther King wrote:

"If a man is called to be a street sweeper, he should sweep streets as Michelangelo painted, or Beethoven composed music, or Shakespeare wrote poetry. He should sweep streets so well that all the hosts of heaven and earth will pause to say, here lived a great street sweeper who did his job well."

Today I shall demonstrate P.R.I.D.E. in everything I do.

SECTION FIVE

The World Loves Dreamers

Dreams are spiritual fuel. When you dream you fan the flames of your imagination. As you pursue your dreams you live a life others fantasize about. The readings in this section gently nudge you to dream big; take the initiative to pursue them; play hard, have fun and never quit.

24: Dream Big Dreams

You can be anything in this world you want, "So what do you want to be when you grow up?" Parents, teachers, and coaches have inspired children with this question for years. It's the key that unlocks the door to creativity and encourages them to dream about their future.

Children walk on the moon; sing at the Met; play baseball at Busch Stadium; perform miracle surgeries; invent things to save the world, and win Olympic gold medals. So, why don't adults dream more? What is there in adulthood that discourages our dreaming? Is it the disappointments along the way? Is part of the rites of passage that we put aside childlike things? Or, do we allow cynicism to influence our *dreamability?*

Children teach us much about dreaming. What if we lived by the question, "What if?" What if we lived by pursuing our dreams versus avoiding our nightmares? We still have the mental faculties to dream. We do it every night.

Dream big dreams. The bigger the better. The world would be lost without dreamers. Dreams offer hope, inspire action, and fuel passion. They add meaning and purpose to daily living. Goals come from dreams. The only thing that limits us is the edge of our imaginations. We place limits on ourselves when we stop dreaming.

Ghandi wrote:

"Man often becomes what he believes himself to be. If I keep telling myself that I cannot do a certain task I may really become incapable of performing the task even though at the beginning I may have had the talent. On the other hand, if I tell myself I can do something I shall surely acquire the capacity to do it even if I didn't have it at the beginning of the task."

Your achieving is tied to your believing. Your abilities will stretch to your capacity for believing.

Why would your Creator give you the ability to dream without the capacity to realize it? He doesn't play these types of games with our minds. He gives us dreamability to add hope and enthusiasm to our lives. Dreams are the stuff life is made of.

Few of us ever really tap into that vast reservoir of potential. Wouldn't it be disappointing, as you're writing that final chapter of your life, to discover a Reader's Digest-condensed story versus a War and Peace-length novel? Each of us has a great story in us. A long, exciting novel filled with passion and hope. You write this story with your dreams.

I was sharing this philosophy with a friend and she said, "Don't you think that's a bit rosy!"

My response was, "Sure! But what's the alternative? Negativism?"

Allow yourself the luxury of conscious dreaming. Give your mind permission to wander the vast plains of your imagination. Treat yourself to a journey of the mind where your imagination links with hope and results in a dream. You are special. Your dreams are special.

Dream big dreams. Sing at the Met. Play a round of golf at the Master's. Play a match at Wimbeldon. Write a Pulitzer-winning novel. Paint a Madonna. Dream your dream. A great big one. Big enough to make your blood race through your veins. Dream something so big that it brings out your best you. Create your own personal field of dreams and play a full nine innings. Dream as a child dreams: simple and wonderful. Dream often. Lose yourself in your dreams. And most importantly, find yourself in your dreams.

Today I shall dream big dreams.

25: So Many Dreams, So Little Time

Why don't more people achieve greatness? This is especially curious when you look at all the ways in which many people succeed today.

The formula appears simple: dream, plan, execute, and enjoy results. It could be a breakdown in one of these areas.

You must have a dream. It all begins here. Goals are signposts along the journey. Dreams are bigger. Unfortunately, some people don't dream. Maybe no one encouraged them to dream. They didn't know it's okay to feel hope.

Some people go through life day-to-day. They focus on daily maintenance issues: eating, sleeping, working, breathing, and so on. They don't have a dream. They make up life as they go along. They're unsure where they're headed and get there a day at a time. You know who they are. Ask the question, "What are your dreams?" They grimace and you both know why. They're good, solid, hard-working people. They lack the dream.

Some people lack resources: the time, money, or support systems that make it easier for them to pursue the dream. Ironically, resources are the easiest to get with a little work and a lot of persistence.

Some lack the ability. Yet, there are thousands of stories of those who lacked the ability and somehow discovered a way to make it happen. They bridged the gap with motivation.

No plan. Some lack a strategy to get there. How many accidental successes do you know? Successful people have detailed a course of action and stick to it. They focus on the dream and avoid distractions along the way.

No guts. The world is filled with people who enjoy visions of success but fall short when it comes to pursuing them. They're strong on dreaming but weak on execution. They're always getting ready to get ready. Like the old saying goes, "No guts. No glory."

No opportunity. It's difficult to believe that in our country someone could say there are no opportunities. Some argue that opportunities for all exist in principle but not in practice. All one needs to do is drive through any town, suburb, or countryside and witness a nation dotted with entrepreneurial dreams. From wing shacks to computer stores. From fast foods stops to auto speed shops. From gas stations to massage parlors. The dream of enterprise is alive in America.

So why don't more people experience the full success within them? I believe it really boils down to dreams. You must have them. Dream until your heart thunders in your chest and your bones itch. Have lots of dreams. Wear the title "Dreamer of many dreams." And then live the motto: "So many dreams, so little time."

Today I shall dream freely.

26: Initiative

Since 1981, I've trained over one hundred thousand salespeople and managers and witnessed some amazing success stories along the way. It's been fascinating to identify what makes high achievers successful.

From the start I've noticed a very special characteristic: initiative. It's fundamental to success in any endeavor. High-initiative people have an internal kick starter. They realize that this is a do-it-to-yourself world, not a dress rehearsal.

High-initiative people don't wait for a problem to become an issue. They nip it in the bud. They're proactive. They don't wait to be told to read a book on their profession. They take the initiative and purchase it. They're out front of the pack. And you know the old saying, "If you're not the lead dog, the view never changes!"

Simple Psychology

My nine year old son, Andrew, oozes initiative. I was in my study at home one day during the summer. He walked in and said, "Dad, I need five bucks to go to Pizza Hut with my buddies."

"Didn't you go to Pizza Hut yesterday with your buddies?" I responded.

"Yeah Dad. That was then but this is now. Come on Dad, give me five bucks."

"Andrew, I can't give you five dollars every day to go to Pizza Hut with your friends. Do you think money grows on trees?"

"Not in this house it doesn't!" he joked.

"You're right." I said.

"Do you have any jobs I can do?"

"No. Not really."

"Well, then, just give me the five bucks."

"Andrew, I told you—I'm not giving you the money."

He left and I thought we were finished. So I returned to the manuscript I was editing.

Within a few minutes, he was back. He placed four stapled index cards on my desk. On the front in big crayon letters it read, "Coupon Book."

I smiled and asked, "What's this?"

He said, "It's a coupon book."

"I can see that. What's it for?" I went along.

"It's good for one car wash and two motorcycle washes. Your cars and motorcycles aren't dirty today, but they will be in a couple of days. So, I'll sell you this for five bucks, what do you say, Dad?"

"Give me two—one for me and one for your Mom." I said handing Andrew a ten-dollar bill.

He left the room smiling and bouncing, and I sat back to consider what just happened.

I was one proud father. This is initiative. It's the trait I see in the successful people I know. If I could just bottle this stuff, I could sell it by direct mail and finish this manuscript on a beach in the Bahamas.

Ironically, I was editing a piece on initiative!

Today I shall use initiative to help me achieve my goals.

27: Everyone Needs A Push

Mother eagles may nudge their offspring to encourage them to fly even when the eaglets may not share the mother's confidence. It's natural to resist leaving the nest. Humans aren't much different. We all need a periodic nudge to get moving.

I was having lunch with a speaker friend and said to him, "You're really up there with the big boys, aren't you?" referring to his success in this industry. He responded, "Yeah, it's great to know that others have done what I'm trying to achieve."

I thought about this for the next few days. He was right. How many times have you done something because someone charted unknown waters and demonstrated that the sailing was fine. This is positive modeling behavior. They do it; you admire their efforts; and say to yourself, "If So and So can do it, why not me?"

When you plan a new venture, it helps to discover that others have made this trip. If your sister continues her education with law school, does it embolden you to pursue your CPA? Her confidence and initiative are contagious.

This is okay. Some people need a catalyst to get started. Watching another stretch or grow can be an incentive for you—even if it is your kid sister.

Parents may or may not be the best source of encouragement as children reach the teenage years. If parents nudge too hard, adolescents may respond opposite to the parents' wishes. They rebel for the sake of rebelling. The parents' response makes the opposite behavior more exciting than it actually is.

Getting a nudge from positive role models is a great way to motivate yourself. You make a friend; become a peer; and maybe find a mentor—someone to help you during tough times.

If another's success inspires you, enjoy the emotion and use it. Emulating their success is a way to express your appreciation for their help.

So, if your younger sister goes to law school and it causes you to turn up the burners on your own life, be grateful. Get your ego out of it. And when you reach full maturity, take her out to lunch and thank her for the powerful example she set for you.

Today I shall give myself a gentle push.

28: Play Hard, Have Fun, and Never Quit

Before the soccer game I told my team, "Stay focused and don't take these guys for granted." We beat this team soundly earlier in the season 4-1. It could have been a rout, but I held back a bit in the end by playing my second and third lines in the more critical positions. I don't like blowouts in kids' sports so I coached them to a 4-1 vs. a 7-1 win. The stage was set. The team knew it would triumph.

At half time I said something like, "I'm pretty upset that the better team isn't winning this game. You guys are better than that." We were losing 3-0. The team agreed that we should be performing better than that. I reminded them of another game we were losing at half time 3-0, and we came back to win it 5-3. The half-time motivational talk worked: they were fired up. They ran onto the field and I knew the second half would be better than the first.

We took the ball from the other team and scored immediately. We were on a roll! Then, something funny happened. The other team responded with a goal of their own—now, a 4-1 game. My team was shocked and never fully recovered. We suffered the worst defeat from a team we had generally beaten. Anything can happen in sports. It still smarts when I think about it.

I reflected on this all week knowing that at the next game I would have to say something to energize this team. My message was simple. "Men, there are only three things we must remember when we are in a game: play hard; have fun, and never quit. None of those happened last week.

"If we play hard during the whole game, we'll discover how good we are. If we don't, we'll always wonder. You owe it to yourselves to discover how good you really are. Aren't you curious about your potential? I know how talented you are! It's you who must discover that.

"We must have fun. None of us does this for any other reason than fun. That is our only reason for being here. If we're not having fun, something is wrong and it may have to do with how much or little we're putting into it. Let's make this thing fun today. And make it fun with your positive energy.

"Never quit. When we're winning we must play even harder so that the other team doesn't catch up. Stay vigilant. And if we're losing we must never quit. Even if the score is overwhelming, play for pride. Let them know you showed up today. Give them a good game. They will respect you. And you will respect yourselves."

I could see the fire in their eyes. At eleven and twelve they understood the simplicity of this message. We won that game 4-0.

I've thought a lot about this message since that gloomy Saturday blowout. It's become a metaphor for how I've chosen to approach most things in my life. Work and play hard. Don't die wondering how good you could have been. Have fun doing it—fun is the primal motivator in life. Never quit. Persistence is a virtue. Who would have thought I was designing this message for me, too?

Today I shall play and work hard, have fun, and never quit.

SECTION SIX

Personal Performance

The proliferation of self-help books, tapes and seminars is proof-positive that most people want to perform at a higher level. These readings offer you some ideas how to compete better with yourself; master the performance formula; develop positive habits, and release the high achiever in you.

29: How To Compete

Because of my work with salespeople and coaching children's athletics, competitiveness is a big part of my life. People tend to compete in one of two ways: with each other or against oneself.

Externally competitive people view competitors with great scrutiny. They ask and answer the question, "What must I do to beat this person?" Their primary concern is the distance they must travel to meet or beat the other person. Companies do it all the time. They seek ways to equal and then surpass the competition.

"To compete in this industry we must be as good as or better than our competition." That's the rallying cry at most business meetings I attend. Some athletes compete this way also. They measure their progress by the scoreboard at the end of the game.

In fact, many coaches prescribe playing against someone who is better than you at a particular sport so that you'll grow. What they fail to tell you is that the real benefit of this exercise is to let you know that higher proficiency is possible. It's a quick and useful benchmark. Unfortunately, for too many it's also the upper limit of performance.

There is another group of competitors who are internally competitive. They compete against themselves, not others. Every once in a great while I hear a company speech that goes like this: "Ladies and gentlemen, keep one ear to the ground but listen attentively to your inner voice. We compete against ourselves. Our obsession is to improve continuously. Let's determine how good we really are." What a great message!

This plays to one of the most fundamental laws of human nature. If my performance standard is external, I look outside of myself and limit myself by my competitor's best game. If I compete with you and my goal is to beat you, what happens when I achieve that goal? Yes, I beat you, but did I determine how good I was along the way? Did I achieve my potential or merely beat you?

The danger of being externally competitive is that I may not discover how good I am—only what it takes to beat someone else. Externally competitive people are running away from something while internally competitive people are running toward something. Internally competitive people recall the best they had—the day they were at their peak—and that becomes the standard by which they judge themselves.

When my son, Paul, plays golf with me, he lives every son's dream: "I must beat Dad." At times I see his frustration. One day I said, "Paul, let's say you're shooting your best round of golf of the year, five strokes below your best score, and I still score lower than you, how would you feel?"

He said, "Disappointed I guess."

I asked, "What if you were playing by yourself and shot that round of golf?"

He smiled and said, "Dad, I'd feel great—like a pro!"

"So who's your real competition?" I asked.

"Me, Dad, not you. I've always got to play my best game not yours. But I still want to beat you." I smiled. Maybe that's a natural thing with boys and dads.

Paul understood clearly. If he shot his best round and I still won, he could feel great about his performance because it was *his* personal best. For me, that was the mental groundwork I needed to lay for the future. With his gift at golf, the day will come when his personal best and mine will collide. His future in golf is different than mine.

Competing against others is helpful because it stirs the competitive juices. It's a standard to beat. But, it falls short of your best you. That's a special type of competitor—one who listens to the inner voice that says, "You're better than that." "You can go where others have never been." "Feel good about what you did today because you brought out your best you." Your inner champion has a great message if you'll listen to the voice.

Today I shall compete with myself.

30: Phenoms and Fundamentalists

I first learned about phenoms and fundamentalists while coaching children's sports. Phenoms are the superstars who perform effortlessly. They make it look easy because of the natural talent they possess. These are also the most highly visible players, and the ones the children try to emulate.

Fundamentalists are the majority in any field—the ninety-plus percenters who manage to get the job done in a big way. They practice and work hard at the fundamentals of their profession. Their talent comes from the application of skills.

There are both in every profession. Some perform so naturally that it appears they were put on this earth to do only that. And then there are the rest of us who must work at what we do, plugging along and still doing the job in a big way.

When I first got into sales I was pretty intimidated by the naturals—the phenoms who, by their personalities or presence, seemed to get orders. I never felt comfortable with that approach because I knew it wasn't me. If I were to enjoy success in sales, I would have to work daily very hard at the fundamentals. I was *then*, and *still* am, a fundamentalist. I continue to work very hard at the basics of selling, speaking, and writing.

The hype and press that surround phenoms mislead us. When a player swings a bat with unconventional motion and sends the ball out of the park, children model that behavior. They learn bad habits. The uniqueness of this player's swing works *only* for him.

A golfing legend with a flying elbow in his swing gives permission to struggling players to do the same. Unfortunately, these struggling players may not possess the special talent to auto-correct for this errant swing behavior.

A tennis player with an unconventional serve is a

poor role model for others attempting to learn the game. The neophyte will stumble as he models the professional's style.

I'm not denigrating the success of our superstars. I'm as impressed by them as the next person. I only point out that many more people could enjoy their talents if they were to look inward versus outward. Develop your gifts by practicing solid fundamentals.

In every profession, there are basic skills to master and fundamentals to internalize. Practice these until they become automatic. Whether it's writing, golf, sales, teaching, or attaching widgets to wadgets, your profession has fundamentals of success.

You can experience wonderful success in whatever you do if you work at these fundamentals. Understand them. Immerse yourself totally in their practice. Master them. For the majority of people reading this, you must concentrate on becoming a fundamentalist. Enjoy watching and learn from the phenoms. And when it comes time to perform, concentrate on the fundamentals to unleash your special talent.

Today I shall practice the fundamentals of my job.

31: The Performance Formula

The most significant day of my education was in a graduate psychology course when the professor wrote this formula on the chalkboard... **P = M x A**

"Ladies and gentlemen, your performance is a function of your motivation and your ability. This is a true mathematical relationship in which one variable compensates for the other."

As I sat there listening to this, I hardly contained myself because of the possibilities I considered. How many people are ten's in ability, but two's or three's when it comes to motivation? The world is filled with unmotivated smart people.

On the other hand, there are many low-ability people who score fifteen on a ten-point motivation scale! The possibilities are exciting. You can be an average ability person and still be a high achiever because of your motivation.

There's more good news. Ability is subdivided into two categories: innate and acquired. Innate ability is the stuff you're born with . . . your raw talent. It's your genetic predisposition.

The other type is acquired ability. This is what you teach yourself along the way. It's the courses you take, the books you read, and the tapes you listen to. It's self-learning as well as formal education. A great benefit of this type of learning is the positive impact it has on your self-esteem. Acquired ability builds competence and confidence which add to your self-esteem.

There are a number of ways to increase your motivation and ability. You increase your motivation when you stop working for the money and start working for the fun. Become self-employed. Be your own boss. Even if it's not financially possible to quit your job, mentally become your own boss. Focus on meeting your upper level needs for creativity, challenge, autonomy, and esteem. Set goals and challenge yourself. Develop a growth-oriented mindset. Live by the question, "Is this the best I have to offer?"

What you don't know has power over you. Conversely, knowledge brings opportunities, choices, and control. Increase your ability by studying, reading, and interacting with those who encourage you to grow. Study industry publications. Subscribe to and read trade journals. Building a better you must become your personal mission. You are the product you offer the world.

Maximize your strengths while managing your weaknesses. If you dislike reading, buy books on tape. If you're a technological illiterate, buy an inexpensive training video or attend a community college course. The world is expanding rapidly in this area.

Each of us is born with special raw material. It's our genetic make-up. How we use and develop that material coupled with our passion determines our future. You have incredible control over your performance by attending to your motivation and your ability.

P = M x A is a simple formula for spectacular performance.

Today I shall stretch to the outer limits of my potential.

32: Develop Good Habits

Habits. We all have them. Good ones, bad ones, and some we'd not like to think about. We choose the ones we want to live and die with.

For years, I've witnessed successful people work, play, and maintain their success. Their happiness is related more to their habits than to circumstance. I've discovered that I'm most fulfilled when I practice those habits that will help me create the type of life I want to live.

Time to play. We learned it early in life, and we caught on quickly. It was fun, effortless, and self reinforcing. Much of our creativity and spontaneity originated there. We played at home, in school, and after school. We were good at it. Then something happened. We grew up and stopped playing. We need to play more. At home. At work. On the golf course. Off the golf course. Play. Simple play. If you're too busy to play, you're too busy.

Time to pray. Some of the earliest things I memorized were prayers. I was fortunate to grow up in an era and attend a school where our day began with prayer. We prayed before lunch. We prayed at the end of the day. We prayed especially before tests. We prayed before going to bed at night. We prayed at meal times. And sometimes, we even prayed in the evenings as a family. This was something I forgot to thank my parents for. And today, if I start my day without a prayer, I feel the void. So, if you're too busy to pray, you're too busy.

Time for work. Hard work is a great ethic. Smart work is a prudent choice. Hard, smart work is a prescription for success. Every successful person whom I know does both. If you don't work hard and smart, you're too busy being busy.

Time for giving and sharing. This is the time for your family and friends. When we were young, this was easy. It was always our priority to spend more time with friends and family: sleepovers, parties, family vacations, and picnics. Today, we're just too busy. And in the midst of our successes, we crave more time with those people we care most about. If you're too busy for friends and family, you're too busy.

Time to recharge our minds and bodies. Funny. In our early years, we spend a huge portion of our lives learning—twelve to eighteen years for most of us. It's habit-forming. Then we get busy and lose the habit. The same thing applies to our bodies. We may have developed the exercise habit to play better at sports but got sidetracked along the way. How many sustaining, successful people do you know that ignore their bodies and minds? If you're too busy to recharge your body and mind, you're way too busy.

I guess you can see where I'm going with this. Good habits bring you closer to the life you want to live. Poor habits pull you aimlessly in the other direction. If you're too busy to play, pray, work smart, share time with those close to you, or develop your mind and body, you're just too busy.

And you deserve better than that.

Today I shall develop and practice good habits.

33: Are You A High Achiever?

What is your achievement style? What do you expect from yourself? Are you pushing yourself to your upper limits or resting on your laurels?

In schools, we hear the labels underachievers, overachievers, and high achievers. At a gut-level, we all know what they mean. Underachiever is a euphemism for the sluggard who fails to use his potential. This definition is thin and doesn't really address the main issue. For whatever reason, the underachiever expects little and accepts less from himself. He's characterized by low self-expectations. The cause may be low self-esteem or confidence.

He doesn't push himself. He rarely tests his mettle or discovers his potential. It's locked away as one of the great secrets of his life. The remedy is one-part "raise the expectation level" and one-part "build the confidence level." Working on self confidence paves the way for raising one's expectations. Confidence comes from mastery and competence. When someone feels he has the ability to handle that which comes his way, his confidence level is higher and he's willing to risk more.

At the other end of the continuum is the overachiever. This person operates with unrealistically high expectations. Whether it's an inflated notion of what he can accomplish; compensating for insecurity; or overly zealous, "blue-sky" thinking the issue is expecting too much. He attempts to do too much of everything. The result is a lack of focus.

Because he attempts too much, he fails to get depth in any one area. This is the proverbial "biting off more than one can chew." This person doesn't know how good he is in any one area because of the superficial treatment he gives to any one area. The remedy for the overachiever is simple: do more of less! Create more realistic expectations. Attempt to accomplish more of fewer things. There's an amazing peace that goes with your accepting some upper limits on how you focus your attention.

Then there's the high achiever. This person operates with ambitious yet realistic expectations and manageable risks. She achieves more because she's focused and gives herself adequate time and energy to pursue a realistic goal. She knows her strengths and weaknesses. She allocates the appropriate time to fully complete a task. She stretches toward realistic goals. On the other hand, overachievers stretch until they snap. Underachievers fail to stretch.

People fight labels because no one likes to be pigeon holed. Labels are useful insofar as they help us screen data and simplify input. Underachievers are not locked into that lifestyle. They can choose to change. They benefit from raising their expectations and holding themselves to a much higher standard. They need to raise the bar on their performance. Overachievers need to moderate their expectations and do more of less. Their greatest ally is focus. High achievers need to keep on keepin' on!

Today I shall become a high achiever.

SECTION SEVEN

Risk Is A Four-Letter Word

Risk and change go hand-in-glove as two inevitable realities of life. We live with both daily, yet seventy percent of the population is low-risk. These readings encourage you to stretch beyond your comfort zone; take a risk; deal with the sibling fears of failure and success; and embrace change with positive anticipation.

34: Take A Risk

My motivational speech to the soccer team went something like, "Guys, what does it mean if we're not getting a yellow card now and again?"

One of the players responded, "It means we're playing it too safe, coach—not aggressive enough. And we can't win if we don't play full-out." Out of the mouth of a fifth grader came the wisdom of sports psychologists and coaches around the world.

Coaching has taught me as much about life as it has sports. A yellow card in soccer means you're pushing the limits and probably ought to tone it down just a hair. It's a foul for which the referee flashes a yellow card warning. It means, "Watch it." A red card means, "You're ejected." The message to the team was, "If we're not getting one of these once in a while, we're not giving it our full effort and won't know how far we can push it."

In our personal lives if we're not getting the occasional yellow card, chances are we're playing it too safe. We're not taking risks. We're living life safely. People avoid risks for a lot of reasons. They lack confidence about their competence. Someone convinced them years ago to live cautiously. They connect risk with failure. Or, they fear the anxiety that accompanies risk.

The risk I'm speaking about is not the foolish stuff, the dangerous I-dare-you-to-do-something or illegal activities. I'm referring to common everyday risk. Approaching your computer aggressively and risking an error message. Taking the initiative to say "Hello" to someone on an airplane and risking rejection. Making a tough decision at work and risking being wrong. Going for the better job and risking being turned down. Asking Mr. or Ms. Right for a date and risking hearing the word "No." Having a party and risking that no one will show.

If you don't bite off a little more than you can chew, how will you ever know your limits? If you don't take the occasional risk in your job, how will you ever know its boundaries? And if you don't get the periodic yellow card, how will you know how aggressively the ref will let you play the game?

The world needs people like you who will take risks. You need to push the boundaries in your life. You never fully discover the limits of your potential without an occasional risk. As far as the natural anxiety that accompanies the risk, feel it and use it for heightened awareness and productive energy.

There will always be those who caution you to slow down and avoid risk. It's what they do. They are your risk guardians. You need another voice in your head that encourages you to reach and risk. This is your own personal motivational coach telling you it's okay to get an occasional yellow card.

Today I shall face the risk of something I've always wanted to do.

35: If It Ain't Broke, Don't Fix It! Why Not?

This is the philosophy of mediocrity. It's a mindset that suggests not to act on something before its time. Unfortunately, this philosophy too narrowly defines interacting with one's environment as a repairperson versus an artist or an architect. When you have the repairperson's mentality, you wait for problems to surface before acting. With the artist's or architect's mentality, you create. You anticipate and act to create a better solution.

The last few years in the business world have witnessed an explosion of the continuous improvement philosophy. This is the belief that anything can be made better with consistent effort. The key is to remain alert and active. The competition is not static and the world will always change. We know, "The only constant in this world is change."

Those who choose the not-broke-don't-fix-it philosophy are security-driven. They desire security in most of what they do. It's natural and healthy to have security in one's life. We need security. It's a basic human need. Too much results in mental hemorrhoids. Some people say, "Can't you leave good enough alone?" "We always do it this way." "Why change horses in the middle of the stream?"

The inverse of that could be asked, "Why stay with an investment that has gone sour just because you've always put your money there?" "Didn't the horse and buggy offer satisfactory transportation in its day?" "Piston-driven airplanes were one of the most revolutionary concepts of the twentieth century." "Carbon paper works fine except for the mess on your fingers, why would we need an expensive machine that takes a photo copy of a document?"

Get the point? Throughout history, progress has come from pioneers who looked at today through tomorrow's eyes. They've given us medical wonders, better lifestyles, air travel, and friendlier ways to interact with our environment. Their premise is simple: there is always another way to state the problem and view the solution. Maybe we have the best solution in place right now, but the seed of a better discovery is in the works. They enjoy a restless curiosity about a better life.

Today I shall demonstrate the pioneer spirit in all that I do.

36: It's Easier To Ask Forgiveness Than Permission

Having a Jesuit education, I often joke about the Jesuit philosophy, "It's easier to ask forgiveness than permission." When I share this with others, they generally laugh. Is this really a Jesuit philosophy? No, but they enjoy a good laugh as much as the next person.

So what's the point? Does it mean that you can do anything in this world that you want, feign ignorance, and beg forgiveness? No. It doesn't exempt anyone from the law, morality or company policies. It's not a contrarian philosophy.

Simply, it's an active philosophy of living. It's taking the initiative. Waiting for permission to act is reactive. Some people argue that in a big organization you cannot have loose cannons.

So what's wrong with the loose cannon who fires an occasional benign volley to wake up the rest of the group? This is an action-oriented philosophy in which initiative is a catalytic motivator. Leaders must come from somewhere.

Living this philosophy is taking risks. There are times you may go too far. There are other times when you will enjoy the status of a pioneer, a free thinker, or dream maker. These are two sides of the same coin.

This is a frightening concept for many people. How would you rather be known, for your compliance or your initiative? If you're a manager, who would you rather have work for you: proactive employees who take reasonable risks, or those who constantly seek your permission before they act?

As a parent, I don't want my children to play with matches and ask forgiveness when caught. I don't want them engaging in dangerous or wrong behavior. But I do want them to exercise some initiative and make decisions. As a parent, I don't want to spend the rest of my life giving permission. I want my children to be self-reliant, high-initiative, decision-making adults.

The only way that this can happen is if they take

measured risks and make some decisions. I'm their safety net for now. But one day they'll have to walk across the wire without the net. Practice, repetition, and guidance will prepare them.

Take an occasional risk. Act on something when your judgment, good sense, and intuition tell you to act. Listen to your instincts. They know something you might discover by taking the risk.

Today I shall act with purpose.

37: Expect Buffeting Along The Way

One of the inevitable aspects of change is the tension people feel. Building and growing muscle tissue involves a certain amount of stretching. It can hurt. The same thing occurs on a mental level when we change. It's the comfort of the familiar resisting the insecurity of the unknown.

In his first book, Chuck Yeager described what it was like to break the sound barrier. At .9 mach, the split second before he broke through the sound barrier, the airplane began to pitch and yaw. It was some of the worst turbulence he ever experienced. These were the shock waves from the sound barrier bouncing against the plane. It was frightening. The moment he broke the sound barrier, the turbulence subsided. It was the smoothest flying he had ever experienced.

This is a great metaphor for what we experience when we make a decision to change. Change anxiety is as natural as breathing. It's the buffeting that comes from within us and around us.

Internal buffeting is what we feel as a natural consequence of venturing out of our comfort zones. It happens. It's exposure to the unfamiliar. Since it's natural and expected, it doesn't need to overwhelm. Knowing this removes some of the sting.

There is real anxiety associated with change and you have a choice of how you want to use it. First, it can be an inhibiting force—one that pulls you back into your comfort zone. Second, you can use it as fuel for your afterburner—that extra kick of adrenaline to propel you through your personal sound barrier faster.

There is another type of buffeting—external buffeting. It's the turbulence that comes from outside influences. It's the pressure to conform, abide, and comply. It comes from bureaucracy, friends, peers, family members, subordinates, and bosses—anyone who is invested in the status quo.

Anyone who has ever dieted has experienced well-meaning friends (probably overweight) who tell you how ill you look since you started this diet. A spouse who is not growing at the same rate as you're growing may resent your enrollment in continuing education. A friend who is struggling financially may envy your financial success. Your change affects those around you almost as much as it affects you. Keep their reactions in perspective.

Preparation is a big part of dealing with this issue. Anticipate buffeting in a very positive way to avoid it blind-siding you. This does not mean you create it. Accept that it happens. Anticipate internal buffeting and recognize it for what it is: fear of the unknown. Be prepared to use the extra energy positively.

Knowing that your growth beyond the comfort zone affects others prepares you for the onslaught of feedback you'll receive. You may even find some good-natured humor in their reaction.

Physical growth requires stretching and pulling muscles. Emotional stretching is equally demanding. Feeling this energy is a sign that you're an evolving, vibrant organism, fulfilling your destiny. You are exactly where you should be, feeling what you should be feeling. Stretch. Grow. Feel. Enjoy.

Today I shall respond positively to the buffeting I experience.

38: The Fear of Failure

Walter was the kind of person who looked great on paper. His résumé was perfect. His experience impressive. He promised to be a superstar. My friend, Ed, hired him and indeed saw great things in those first few months. After a while, Walter started to play it safe. He made only safe sales calls that promised success. He set unchallenging goals, never stretching to the edge of his potential.

After a few coaching and counseling sessions Ed encouraged him to open up. Walter said, "In college, I was a good baseball player. I played about half the games and sat out the other half. I know I could have been great. But being good was good enough. What if I had tried to be great and couldn't have been? I don't know if I could have taken the blow to my self-esteem. When I was good, I dreamed of being great and that was good enough.

"Ed, selling is a lot like that for me. I am a good salesman. I could be great and I know it. But what would happen if I tried and wasn't great? I couldn't handle that. Dreaming about it is good enough for me."

Walter left after a while for another job where being good enough was acceptable. It's sad that Walter is so afraid of failure he will never discover the outer reaches of his potential. His fear of failure stemmed from his inability to distinguish performance from self-worth. He wasn't able to separate his "being" from his "doing." Your "doing" is secondary to your "being." What you *do* is not who you *are*. People like Walter struggle when their self-worth comes from success on the outside.

Defining oneself in external terms makes self-acceptance conditional on achievement. You never give yourself the permission or the opportunity to fail. And failures teach us important lessons as we integrate them into our personalities: humility, empathy, and patience.

A closely-related fear is another's opinion. "If I try and fail in my attempts, what will others think of me?" Again, the individual ties self-worth to an external standard—someone else's opinion. You are a great person in spite of your successes or failures.

Some people fear failure because they are afraid of discovering that "I may not have what it takes to be successful in this world." This may be connected to self-esteem and how one needs to feel competent in one's environment. Or "having what it takes" sounds like a value judgment to me. It's one of those umbrella clichés people throw around to cover everything from ability to personality. On the other hand, discovering that one may not have what it takes to perform a certain task is perhaps the best thing to determine.

I absolutely do not have the temperament to perform the accounting functions in my business. Could I fail at this task? Yes, very probably, and it would most likely be a self-inflicted wound. Could I succeed at this job? Maybe, but the attention to detail would drive me nuts! In this example, not having what it takes is a blessing for me. I don't want the job.

Finally, there are low-risk individuals who are so afraid of risk that they will attempt nothing that is unproven. There are times when this may be situationally prudent but not as a lifestyle. Failure is a fact that describes performance of a behavior. Any meaning you attach beyond that is editorializing on your part.

No one likes to fail. It can be embarrassing and financially painful. But failing in business or at sports does not mean failing at being a person. The focus must be *who you are* not *what you do*. There are many lessons in failure. It teaches you how to start again. Analyze your failures, don't judge them. It shows you things to avoid doing. It strengthens your resolve if you let it.

Failing now and again reinforces in your mind that you are a doer, a shaker, a mover; one who drives the trends, sets the pace, and goes with the ebb and flow—the risk takers who view defeat as a performance failure, not a person failure.

Life offers many wonderful opportunities. You make a decision to pursue or avoid them. You live in a country where entrepreneurs are encouraged and admired. Being different is okay. Achieving your goals is okay. And the occasional failure is okay. It's a sign that you're reaching—stretching to the outer limits of your potential, and living your destiny. Remember, when you risk, failure is only a small part of the equation. You also risk success.

Today I shall feel the fear of failure and move on.

39: The Fear of Success

Things are going well for you. You just got a promotion at work. The work is challenging, and you're earning more money than you thought was possible. Your spouse is doing well. Your combined income is beyond your wildest imaginings; your marriage has never been better; your children are performing spectacularly in school and sports; you have just been elected chairperson of a social group to which you are very committed; and you are playing four strokes below your golf handicap. With all this wonderful stuff happening in your life, you say to yourself, "I just know . . ."

How did you finish? Did your answer sound like, "Something bad is about to happen"? When I perform this exercise in seminars, I generally hear a chorus of "The other shoe is about to drop" or, "Things never work out for me like this!" I wish you could see their faces as I get about halfway through this exercise. They grin, smirk, and shuffle. Their expressions say it all: "Life never gets this good for me."

Why? Where is it written that life shouldn't be good?

Simple Psychology

Is it nature's law that when great things happen, fate intercedes? Or, is it our doing?

A few years ago Industry Week magazine ran a cover story about this. In it, they disclosed that seventy percent of all successful executives have expressed that at some point in their lives they felt like fakes, that their success really wasn't them.

Are you haunted by your own ambitions? Do your dreams and aspirations scare you? Do you feel anxious when you fantasize about how good things could be? This is the fear of success and it manifests itself in three ways.

First, high expectations. "If I succeed at this task, they'll expect it from me all the time." The irony is jolting. The premise is that your success is a fluke—that you'll be unable to achieve greatness again. Says who?

Success can be an encore performance. Sports teams win back-to-back championships all the time; writers produce consecutive best-sellers; surgeons perform thousands of successful operations—one right after another. You need to rid yourself of this bias. Of course you can do it again, I'd be surprised if you didn't.

Second, separation anxiety. "You know where I've been and who my friends are. If I'm successful, what and whom do I leave behind." Imagine an unrelenting gravitational pull at your current performance level. You fail because you fear others will resent and reject you. You're successful and they're not. Some may resent your success. Others may vicariously live it with you. Some may even actively try to discourage you. Do you really want someone else's insecurities holding you back?

Third, low self-worth. "I don't know that I really deserve success. So many others are struggling out there." Whether it's guilt or a poor self-image, why don't you deserve it, if you're willing to put forth the effort, discipline, and commitment to make it happen? Who, more than you, deserves it? No one. You must not cheat yourself of success on the coattails of someone else's failure. No one knows for sure why another fails as we succeed.

The fear of success is universal. Everyone feels it to varying degrees. To some, it's growth pains. For some, it's down-right scary. To others, it's something in between. Some manage the fear and move on to excel. Others, succumb to it and spend a great deal of their lives wondering, "What if?"

Today I shall pursue the success within me.

40: On The Vanguard Of Change

Change scares a lot of people for a lot of reasons. Some resist because they are drawn out of their comfort zones. Others resist because they fear the unknown. And, in spite of the resistance, change happens. It's all around us.

We change our elected officials every couple of years. Corporations change strategies and structures every few months. And warp-speed technology advancements change the ways we communicate. It's enough to wear you out.

Change has been the only constant throughout time. "You cannot walk into the same river twice," said

Heraclitus. By the time you reach the other bank it has changed. This metaphor is especially relevant today. Today's changes occur at breakneck speed.

There are the leading-edge types: those who ride the waves of change drawing from its momentum. They thrive on change, understand it's dynamics, and wield it to their advantage. There are the passive participants of change, the hangers-on. They wait for the inevitable change to turn into reality and then act. Once they're convinced they must change, they do so albeit reluctantly, longing for the way things used to be.

And then there are the victims—those who get swept away by change. They fight it tooth and nail and in the end, lose to it.

Whether or not you like change, there are consequences. If you decide to join change in its earliest phases, you risk failure and danger. If you join it late, you risk failure by attrition. If you're on the vanguard, you risk the potential early rewards. If you're on the trailing edge, you risk getting what's left by those who pioneered it.

For those who choose to wait, the distance between you and those on the vanguard is great and grows daily. Think of the ground you must gain if you wait too long to make the inevitable changes. Every second you wait and every step forward they take widens the gap. It's not a matter of *if* you'll change. It's *when* you'll change. You must decide how much ground you want to make up.

Today I shall embrace change with positive anticipation.

SECTION EIGHT

How to Get More Out of Life

This sounds like a teaser headline in an ad for a get-rich scheme. The promise is one of life's great paradoxes: the more you put into it, the more you get out of it. These readings offer you some ideas on how to improve your lot in life by putting a lot more into life. They offer tips for blasting out of comfort zones; reaching higher; exercising positive action; and adding more value to what you do.

41: Act Like You're Worth It

In one of my seminars, a salesman told me how his part-time college job impressed upon him a work ethic that he would carry with him and use to create a successful sales career. As a full-time college student, he worked as a part-time welder assistant. He complained to his journeyman mentor about earning a "measly $1.00 per hour" for doing the same work as the experienced welder who earned $1.25 per hour.

The young welder felt he deserved $1.25 also. The older welder said to him, "If you want to earn $1.25 per hour, stop griping about it and act like you're worth it." This was the simple psychology of a hard-working man. The salesman internalized this work ethic and applied it to much of his life. "If I wanted to be an 'A' student I had to study like one. If I wanted to be an 'A' father, I had to act like one. And if I wanted to charge more for my

Simple Psychology

product and get it, I had to be worth more than my competition." This became a forty-year working philosophy for the salesman.

How many people today are willing to pay this price? The world is filled with $1.00 per hour welders who complain about their wages but fail to act like they're worth more. They feel that they should earn the $1.25 for just showing up. Wrong! That's $1.00 an hour thinking. Too many students feel they should receive "A's" without studying. And too many salespeople charge more for their goods and services without offering greater value.

This is profoundly simple psychology. For some, it's an ice-water-in-the-face therapy. Some roll their eyes and raise their eyebrows at this blunt reality. Others welcome its frankness. If you want more from life, put more into it. If you want better grades, study harder. If you want to earn a higher wage, you must work harder. If you want greater job security, you must add more value as an employee. If you want a more attractive body, you must work at it.

It seems that some of life's best education happens outside the classroom from teachers who lack formal education but have seen plenty of life. Imagine meeting your most unforgettable character in a part-time job and having this person say something so profound that it will affect the rest of your life. You've met this person with the help of our friend, the salesman. You, too, can adopt this work ethic as your own.

Today I shall perform at the level of results I desire.

42: Avoid Early Mental Retirement

The salesman said to me, "The most significant motivational talk I've ever heard was thirty years ago. The speaker admonished us not to retire at thirty-five mentally and at sixty-five physically. I've always used that as my personal pep talk."

The simplicity of this inspirational message fascinated me. It's amazing how a few words stick with people and continue to inspire them long after they hear them. I wonder if the speaker understood the impact he had on this man's life.

Early mental retirement is a prescription for failure in any profession. As humans, we are growing, evolving, and emerging organisms. From the moment we are conceived we grow and develop. Our destiny is growth. We are fully alive and enthusiastic when we dig down deep inside ourselves and discover another secret about our ability—another dimension of the human spirit.

Potential is an exciting concept. In those fleeting moments when we catch a glimpse of what we're really capable of doing we thrill ourselves. In the long hours of mental retirement we disappoint ourselves with wasted time and lost opportunities.

People who invest their lives in discovering more about themselves glow with the enthusiasm of a pioneering scientist who just discovered the answer to one of life's most troubling questions. It isn't the money or the fame. It's the discovery of a truth. It's their desperate curiosity about potential that fuels their excitement for life. They live by the question, "Aren't you the least bit curious about your potential and destiny?"

These are the people who never retire mentally.

They may retire physically because of other interests and limitations, but mentally they grow until they die. Their passion for living is contagious. Being around them and sharing their enthusiasm is like a personal motivational rally. They have discovered the greatest secret of them all: you're never quite so alive as when you become more of that which your Creator intended.

Today I shall explore my potential.

43: Blast Out of Your Comfort Zone

What does it mean to be in a comfort zone? Is it possible to be in a comfort zone while living in a world filled with anxieties? Or, are people really deluding themselves?

A comfort zone is a plateau where we stop doing many of the things that made us successful. It's a pause in our forward motion or career momentum. It's a behavioral response to an emotional decision to stay where we are. Beyond this, it's an area of familiarity—something to which we're accustomed. In fact, it may not be comfortable at all—just familiar. This explains why companies continue to buy from a vendor whose service is less than par. They're predictably bad (familiar pain) and the customer adjusts ordering habits accordingly.

Comfort zones are not limited to business. They happen in all areas of our lives. We get comfortable in relationships, take each other for granted and work less hard at them. We may not romance each other the way we once did. We become financially comfortable and are less prudent about investing—our needs are met. We get comfortable spiritually and do not pray as often as we did when our needs were greater. Physically, we may get complacent and turn fat, dumb, and happy as our bodies deteriorate. Comfort zones happen in all areas of our lives. It's not a question of *if*, it's a question of *when*.

Our studies indicate that 25% of all people are in a comfort zone—maybe a parking zone; another 57% are on the fence; and only 18% really test their mettle. Ninety-six point five percent of companies taking part in another study report that plateaued employees are a problem for their organization.

Why do people stay in comfort zones?

Laziness. How many people are really lazy? I'm too optimistic to believe that a significant number of people are lazy. Low self-esteem? Maybe, but not lazy. Discouraged? Yes, but not lazy.

How about the person who is truly comfortable? If you're comfortable and productive, more power to you! You've achieved something to which each of us aspires. Again, I believe that number is low.

What about the person who fears failure? "If I try and fail, I don't know if I can take the blow to my self-esteem." Which is worse—trying and failing or not trying at all? Robert Schuller said, "I would rather attempt a great many things and fail than to attempt nothing and succeed." Failing to try is far worse than the failure to achieve. When you fail to attempt, you go through life wondering what would have happened if you had tried. "Did I have it in me?" "Was I that good?" These unanswered questions haunt people in mid-life.

Simple Psychology

What about the fear of success? How about the person who is frightened by his own ambitions and reluctant to act on them? "What if I try and really blow out this year's sales quota, they'll expect that every year." It's ironic that this person is afraid of pursuing that which he is capable of achieving—his potential.

A common fear of success is the person who recognizes that excelling in one area of his life may distance him from all those around him. It's a form of separation anxiety. And others may even remind him of this distance with good natured fun. "Hey, what are you doing, bucking for a promotion? Slow down. You're making the rest of us look bad."

So, how do you deal with comfort zones? The first step is to ask yourself, "Why am I in one? Am I afraid of failing? Do I hate change? Am I lazy? Am I truly comfortable? Am I afraid of success and if so, why?" Asking and answering these questions is the first step in your blasting out of a comfort zone.

Then, you must accept responsibility for your success. Ninety percent of what happens to you is largely determined by what you do and don't do for yourself. As you seize positive control over your life you will feel the confidence to stretch.

Next, dream big dreams—big enough to cause your heart to pump a little faster. Design goals that will help you reach these dreams. Construct a plan to achieve these goals, and get busy pursuing them.

Today I shall blast out of my comfort zone.

44. Low-Hanging Fruit

Over the years I've heard the term "low-hanging fruit" used in a variety of contexts. I'm unsure when I first heard it, but I believe it was when my family went apple picking at a local orchard. As we collected our baskets and apple pickers an old man who owned the place said, "Go for the higher fruit."

I asked, "What do you mean?"

He responded, "Most people come here and pick the low-hanging fruit. They don't reach for the fruit at the top of the trees even though it gets more rain, greater sunshine and it's closer to the heavens. It's tougher to get to." He smiled, appreciating the wisdom of his metaphor.

I thought about this a lot as we walked around the orchard. He was right. Most people chose the low-hanging fruit. The trees were decorated at the top with plenty of ripe fruit yet picked clean at the bottom.

Over the years I've considered this a great metaphor for many things we experience in life. Salespeople pick low-hanging fruit when they make the easy sales calls and avoid those that are inconvenient to call on. I witnessed this at a customer's office a few months ago when he showed me his "war room"—the office in which he kept a map of his sales region. He marked each customer location with a colored push pin. Not surprisingly, the push pins followed the major highways. And yet he estimated that there were an equal number of opportunities off the beaten path. His sales force was going for the low-hanging fruit, highly-visible easy pickens! What happens to the rest, the higher-hanging fruit? They go largely ignored and under serviced because they're not as convenient to visit. Imagine how rich those other opportunities must be if everyone feels this way.

When brainstorming we may choose the first good idea instead of reaching higher for the next better idea. We may opt for the first easy solution to a problem when a much better solution is available to those who reach a little higher.

Recently in a sales management training session, we were discussing application tips for an action plan when the managers jumped at the first and most obvious ideas. I pressed them further, challenging the group to discover even better ideas. They fell into the trap of picking the low-hanging fruit—the obvious, the highly-visible, and the easy.

In this case reaching higher means going for the less obvious and refusing to settle for the first idea that comes along. In the first highly-visible form, there may be only the seed of something better. We must reach higher for the better solution.

How many times in life do we choose the easy path only because it's convenient? Humans are not genetically encoded to take this path—it's a choice we make. It's the path of least resistance—the low-hanging fruit.

So, what's the message? Use patience and persistence. When you find yourself going for the obvious, the easy and all too commonplace, reach higher. Look for and choose the higher-hanging fruit.

Today I shall reach for the higher-hanging fruit.

45: Do You Add Value Or Cost?

The concept of adding value so intrigues me that I've written three books and dozens of articles on it. Every year, I take my value added message to thousands of people. The message is as relevant for everyday living as it is for business.

Simply, it's a philosophy of maximum performance, not minimum standards. It's challenging yourself with, "Do I add value or cost?" In business, it's the difference between your being a profit center or a cost center for your company. Hint: there's no job security in being a cost center.

In life, it's the difference between what you're contributing and what you're consuming. In a relationship, adding value means giving something to it: time, energy, and love. Adding cost means taking from the relationship. At work or on athletic teams, your energy either adds to the group's momentum or it's a resistance force on the group.

The value adding philosophy is a mindset or an attitude toward life. If you accept this philosophy, you're a pay-the-price kind of person. When the attitude is in place, the behavior is free. People who believe in this philosophy naturally behave in ways to support it.

On the other hand, if you're adding cost, you're doing just enough to get by. Just-enoughs live the philosophy of minimum standards. You're coasting. And there's only one way to coast—downhill!

To add value, you must first define life in terms bigger than yourself—to believe that you're a viable part of a society greater than one. Viable means you add to it. This is completely different than someone who drains and draws from society.

Chief Seattle (1852) said:

"This we know: the earth does not belong to man, man belongs to the earth. All things are connected like the blood that unites one family. Man did not weave the web of life, he is merely a strand in it. Whatever he does to the web, he does to himself."

Each of us has a destiny in life—a talent or skill we contribute to humanity. It's our gift to a society that gives to us. Adding value is the natural expression of what you were put on this earth to do. Those who add value at work, home or church discover one of the most basic truths in life: the more you give the more you get. It's nature's law of reciprocity. It's another way of saying, "What goes around comes around."

So, the question to challenge yourself with daily is, "Am I adding value or cost?" If your answer is, "Adding cost," look for ways to contribute. If your answer is, "Adding value," keep on, keepin' on!

Today I shall add value in all things I do.

46: Positive Action: Get Busy

Some people spend way too much of their lives thinking and planning versus doing and pursuing. This is paralysis by analysis: analyzing something to death. They're getting ready to get ready. It's procrastination and it helps them avoid risk or failure. They fail to realize that nothing happens until they act, and a decision to do nothing is still a decision to do something. It's de-

Simple Psychology

ciding on indecision.

At age eight my daughter understood the importance of action. I was at Amanda's soccer game. It was the third quarter and her team was winning 2-0. She had scored both the goals. (You tell me who the best kid on the team was!) Amanda was sitting on the sidelines with a long face so I went over and said, "Honey, what's wrong?"

"Oh Daddy, the coach pulled me out."

I responded with, "That's okay Amanda, this is a training league. Everyone needs a chance to play. It's the fair way to do things." I felt smug knowing that I approached it thoughtfully and maturely.

She corrected, "Daddy, you don't understand."

"Sure I do. This is the third quarter. You kicked two goals and the coach is resting your foot for the last quarter when you'll come in and kick a couple more to put this game away." I was really proud now because I explained it from the coach's view-point, having coached soccer for years myself. Now, she'll understand the wisdom of winning as only an adult can explain it.

"Daddy, you still don't understand!"

"All right, Amanda, what don't I understand?"

"Dad, you don't kick goals if you're not in the game!"

"You don't kick goals if you're not in the game," I thought to myself.

I stared at her and said, "Amanda, people pay me a lot of money to say that kind of stuff."

She looked at me and grinned. The wisdom of an eight-year-old—you don't kick goals if you're not in the game. Action is the name of the game. "Dad, I'd rather score a goal than talk about it any day."

This is the same child who years later, at age ten,

when asked if she ever dreamed about being successful in life responded with, "Sure I dream about it. But, more importantly, I *plan* to be successful."

When I asked her to expound she said, "Dad, if I only dream about it, it may never happen. If I plan it and act on it, I can make it happen."

This was a clear-thinking child teaching an old dog new tricks. In her own way and in her own words, Amanda figured it out. Planning is important, but *action* brings the payoff. At some point, we must stop planning and start doing. Even the old saying, "Measure twice, cut once," stresses action. Positive thinking without positive action is positive stinking. Instead of getting ready to get ready, a better attitude is to get ready and get busy.

Today I shall act with purpose.

47: There's No Traffic Jam On The Extra Mile

One of the advantages of my job as a professional speaker is that I meet successful people. I also meet people at the other end of the success-failure continuum. From this, I've identified two types of people: *extra milers* and *just-enoughs*.

The *extra miler* makes success a habit. It's a way of life, a philosophy, an attitude, not an event. The *extra miler* understands that success in any venture happens on purpose with purpose. It's no accident.

The *extra miler* lives on the edge of human potential. She understands that the difference between ordinary and extraordinary performance is the little something extra she gives.

The *just-enough* operates within a comfort zone of self-imposed upper limits. He succeeds for a while and coasts for a while. He does just enough to get by. He sells just enough to keep the wolves away from the door. He does just enough paper work to keep the boss off his back.

The *extra miler* has the attitude of gratitude. He uses a unique prism to view life. He views it positively. He looks for the greater good in all situations and chooses not to focus on the negative. He learns from the bad while focusing on the good.

Failure doesn't inhibit the *extra miler* from trying again. She gives failure the appropriate amount of emotion and moves on to better things. To the *extra miler*, life's greatest failure is quitting the race because she didn't win the first lap.

A second thing that characterizes the *extra miler* is positive action. Positive attitude without positive action is only half the answer. The *extra miler* believes that one must be active to be successful. To win the race, you've got to be in the race.

The human race is a lot like a horse race. If you want to cross the finish line as a champion, you've got to perform like one. It is a unique combination of your high level of initiative coupled with everyone else's inertia, apathy and indifference that will make you successful.

The third thing that characterizes the *extra miler* is positive control. The *extra miler* exerts maximum positive control over her life. She's internally driven. She's the captain of her ship, the master of her fate, and the architect of her future.

The *extra miler* accepts responsibility for the present and the future. The *extra miler* avoids saying things like, "With the economy so bad, I just can't sell!" Instead she says, "I know things are bad for some people, but I don't think I'll participate in a bad economy. I'll create a good one for me."

The *extra miler* replaces the words fate and luck with commitment and determination. She replaces *I can't* with *I won't*. And she says *when* versus *if*.

There is no heavier burden than a great opportunity. As you read this you either have a great opportunity or a tremendous burden, depending on your perspective. And still each of us must make a conscious choice as to how we plan to spend the remaining time we have on this earth. Remember, there's no traffic jam on the extra mile!

Today I shall become an extra miler!

48: The Grass Is Always Greener

I was in my backyard last evening admiring my neighbor's lawn, imagining how nice it would be if my lawn looked half as good as his. It's a beautifully thick, well-manicured, weedless, Bermuda carpet. It should be on the cover of a horticulture magazine. Why is his grass greener than mine? Isn't that always the case?

An early human phenomena is the tendency to want what someone else has. A baby watches his mother prepare a bottle, and he cries for it. A child plays with a toy, and a sibling wants it. This persists throughout life. The grass always looks greener in your neighbor's yard.

I like your sports car and try to convince my wife that it would be a prudent investment for us. At a business meeting, I so admire your fountain pen that I buy one just like it. Your briefcase must be the secret of your amazing success. I've got to have one.

Your job appears to be much more challenging and meaningful than mine. Your spouse does more for you than mine does for me. You're such a lucky person. I know our vacations could be as entertaining and relaxing as yours if we had a second home in that part of the country. Your friends are exciting. And the way you dress is so fashionable I feel like I'm behind the times.

One of the incontrovertible truths of life is that many times, your stuff looks better than my stuff. Fundamentally, the issue is simple. When I focus on what I have, I'm satisfied. When I focus on what you have, I'm restless. I have fun when I play with my toys and feel envy as I preoccupy myself with your toys. I feel rich when I concentrate on what I have and poor when I focus on what I don't have.

Time spent envying your lawn is wasted. I may not know the price you paid for it. Your sexy sports car may have an incredibly rough ride. Your elegant fountain pen may leak and ruin a sixty dollar dress shirt. Your leather briefcase may be so heavy that you suffer tendinitis in the elbow from carrying it. Your job's greatest challenge could be balancing your travel with family events. Your spouse may have horrible breath and snore like a freight train. Your vacation home may have termites and sit on a toxic waste site. Your stylish clothes may fit so poorly that you're in misery every time you button your pants. And your friends may be so superficial that you don't trust a one. In short, your grass may not be as green as it looks.

Or, it may be greener because you spend more time working on it. Your sports car may shine more because you polish it each weekend. Your job may be more challenging because you put your whole heart and soul into it. Your relationship with your spouse may be great because of what you do for him or her behind the scenes. And your appearance may have everything to do with the amount of time you invest at the fitness center.

And so I came to the conclusion that the reason Dave's lawn looks so much better than mine is that he spends endless hours each week weeding, pruning, fertilizing, trimming, and mowing. And while he's doing this, I'm on my motorcycle exploring the turns and twists of Missouri's back roads. Funny, though. He came over to my house a little later asking to sit on my bike. Hard to figure, eh?

Today I shall focus on what I have, not what I don't have.

SECTION NINE

Motivation

Motivation, like much of life, is a do-it-to-yourself thing. It starts with a need, want, or desire and manifests itself in behavior. The readings in this section clarify some of the most widely-held beliefs and misconceptions about money, jobs, values and motivation.

49: Confusing Values With Motivation

People come to our seminars confusing motivation with values. This is especially true of managers as we're discussing incentive programs and how to motivate salespeople. They say things like, "Our salespeople should be more money motivated than they are."

I generally respond, "Why?"

To which they reply, "Because that's what motivates good salespeople." See what I mean about values? This confusion between values and motivation generally begins with an *oughta* or *shoulda*.

To understand your personal motivation, know what you stand for—your values. The core elements of your motivation and behavior are values. You move toward that which you value and away from that which has little value to you. Values are your moral compass. They guide your journey.

A clearer understanding of your values makes it easier to set priorities. You have a better perspective when to say "Yes" and "No." Another benefit of understanding your values and the uniqueness of your priorities is that you gain an appreciation for other peoples' values. This means being less judgmental about things.

These questions will help you better understand why you do what you do:

What makes your blood race through your veins? What really excites you? What will cause you to get out of bed at four a.m.? Golf? Fishing? Vacation? Work? Will you do it without an alarm clock?

If I could do it all over again, I wish I would have spent more time . . . Identify what's missing in your life. Some may respond with "more time on the job" if they feel they retired too early mentally and could have experienced greater success and satisfaction in their careers. Most will probably respond with something like a hobby or family time. Wouldn't it be a shame to ask that question too late in life?

What six things do I value above and beyond all other things in this world? List the six most important things in this world to you and why. What would you give your life for? Who are the people in this world that mean the most to you?

If you had just thirty days to live, how would you use that time? It would be interesting to fill that month. Why wait for doomsday to do it? Some people may spend more time at the beach with their families. Others might take the trip they've always wanted to take. Another might read a book that's been collecting dust for the past few years. And someone may finish writing the book he or she set aside.

Answer these questions to understand yourself better. Connect with your values. Study them. Let them guide your motivated behavior.

The most highly-confident, focused, and committed people I know are those who understand what would cause them to walk across a bed of hot coals. They know what they value and live their lives accordingly. What do you value that much?

Today I shall clarify my values and let them guide my actions.

50: Intrinsic Versus Extrinsic Motivation

Psychologists have conceived of a number of theories to explain why people behave in certain ways. Some focus on the *what* that motivates individuals: money, praise, and titles. Maslow's Hierarchy of Needs model is an example of these content models of motivation.

Another school of thought is process models. These focus on the decisions people make about engaging in certain behavior. The decisions are based on perceptions and expectancies for success. Simply, people try if they feel they have a reasonable chance for success, perceive few obstacles, and the behavior has a valued payoff.

There are behaviorists like Pavlov and Skinner who believe that behavior is maintained by its consequences. Define the behavior, and shape it with a reinforcement schedule that encourages repetition.

Each school of thought presents convincing arguments to support their premise. In this motivational mire is the concept of intrinsic and extrinsic motivation. Extrinsic rewards come from outside the behavior: the pay, praise, titles, promise of a better job, a corner office, or the proverbial gold watch at retirement. This is external reinforcement.

Intrinsic rewards come from within the behavior: fun, challenge, the opportunity to express oneself creatively, freedom to explore, satisfaction from a job well-done—the intangibles.

Some people are extrinsically motivated. Others are intrinsically motivated. Extrinsically-motivated people view behavior (the job) as a means to get what they *really* want: the praise or the recognition. Intrinsically-motivated people find it difficult to separate the behavior (the job) from the reinforcer: the joy of doing it. They do it because it's fun. They do it because it's challenging, and it gives them an opportunity to test themselves.

Two prescriptions emerge from this. First, know what motivates you. What makes your blood race through your veins? What gets you out of bed in the morning? Is it the money, fun, challenge, independence, recognition from your boss, or to provide for your family?

Second, look for ways to enrich your job. How can you make it more challenging, demanding of your creativity, and open to your input? The more of you that *you* build into your job, the more intrinsically satisfying it is. You can't wait to do the job!

You might be saying to yourself, "Tom, that's easy for you. You're self-employed. You can do anything you want." So can you.

Make an appointment with your boss. Offer suggestions for enriching your job. With the spotlight today on empowerment and re-engineering, now is the ideal time to create your own job. Offer reasons on how this will have a positive impact on your company. Tie it to productivity. Reasonable managers will understand. It will be a win-win solution.

Today I shall work as if I were self-employed.

51: Money and Motivation

Do you want to discover what motivates you? Answer this question: *What does money buy me?*

Managers and business owners complain that if their salespeople would only work a little harder, they could earn more money. Management struggles with why some blue collar workers refuse to work overtime and earn big money. The answer is simple. People don't work for money. They work for what it buys them. Money is not the universal motivator. Some people would rather have time off as an incentive.

In psychological terms, money is a secondary reinforcer. A secondary reinforcer enables you to get what you really want, the primary motivator. In experimental labs, monkey's work for secondary reinforcers—tokens they use to buy food.

Teachers use this method also. Students work for stars that can be used for candy or some other purpose.

Let's return to the original question. What does money buy you? That's your primary motivator. If it buys you things, you're motivated by material items. You like nice stuff. If it's a way for you to keep score, you're power motivated. You earn more money than I do; therefore, you win, in your opinion. Does money buy security? If so, you're security motivated. You feel secure when you earn and save money. Maybe it's a prestige thing with you. You like being affluent because others admire you for that. You're people motivated.

Some entrepreneurial type reading this is thinking to himself/herself, "I like money because it buys me independence." These folks like the freedom of calling their own shots. The money is good, but it's secondary. Some work for money because it meets their basic essentials for life: food, shelter, clothes, etc. Others think of money in retirement terms. They want to be independent of their children.

It's important to understand what money buys you because it provides clearer insight into your motivational profile. Over half of the people with whom I work cannot tell me what motivates them. They generally respond with the perfunctory answer, "Money motivates me." It sounds good, but it's too shallow to understand oneself better.

If you understand why you're really working, perhaps there's another way to infuse your job with more of it. If you do that, you'll stay focused and satisfied. The money is a nice, secondary benefit.

Today I shall explore and develop my motivational profile.

Simple Psychology

52: Is Your Job Motivating?

"How can I get maximum performance from my employees?" This is a frequently-asked question I hear in my management course. Every manager wants the magic motivation pill—to clearly understand what motivates someone to do something. There is no magic motivation pill. However, there are some questions you must ask yourself regarding your career.

Is it fun? Think about the last time you had difficulty sleeping because you were excited about your plans for the next morning. Fun is the primal motivator. Children play because it's fun. What if you could redesign your job to make it more fun? What would make going to work in the morning more fun? Take that idea to your boss.

Is it challenging? Everyone likes to test his mettle. Too much challenge overwhelms and too little under utilizes and bores. Jobs that give you an opportunity to stretch bring out your personal best. Watch for boredom and frustration. Each signals a different message about the degree of challenge in a job. Stretch don't snap. Pursue more or less challenge in your job.

Is it mine? When you put your fingerprints all over the job, you're more excited about doing it. Go for more latitude, authority, and freedom to explore. It satisfies your need for autonomy. It's difficult to explore one's potential without freedom. When you feel empowered and have the opportunity to achieve excellence, you display your personal best. Discuss this with your boss.

Is it meaningful? Most jobs can be made meaningful when one fully understands its importance. Prove to yourself the vital role your job plays in the company.

What you do matters. Pursue meaningful activities in your job. Focus on priorities.

Is it equitable? Are you getting as good as you're giving? Everyone wants equity. People balance their inputs and outcomes. If there's equity between your giving and getting, you're motivated to perform. If you want to earn more, put more of yourself into the job. If you're not getting as good as you're giving, approach your boss.

Am I needed? Do you play an important role in the business? This is similar to meaningfulness. When you're needed and feel you belong, you contribute to the team. Everyone wants to feel that they are part of something bigger than themselves. We is greater than me!

Am I recognized? Your contributing is important. Being recognized for it is even better. This is more than the fifteen minutes of stardom Andy Warhol talked about. This is the ongoing praise and recognition for a job well done. Seek feedback on your performance. Get recognized. You may need to be better at asking for it than your boss is at giving it.

I finished each of these key points with an action tip for you. Because motivation is an internal process, you are responsible for your behavior. If you ask these seven questions and are dissatisfied with the answers, *you* are the one who must initiate the change. *You* are responsible for your career. Your boss does not motivate you—*you* motivate *you*!

Today I shall make my job more motivating.

53: Real-World Motivation

Motivation fascinates some people while confounding others. It has inspired abundant research resulting in diverse psychological theories. In spite of the varied schools of thought, there are some basic truths about motivation.

First, you cannot motivate another person. That sounds odd from a motivational speaker. From my professional studies, I know that motivation is an internal force. It comes from within the individual and impels action. The best we can hope to achieve is to create an environment that stimulates another's internal motivation.

When I meet resistance to this idea in a seminar I ask, "Do you believe you can lead a horse to water but can't make him drink it?" Most people agree. What if you ran the horse hard or salted its food? The horse is thirsty and feels the need to drink. The motivation comes from within the horse based on your changing its environment. Your goal must be to provide an environment that induces motivated behavior.

Second, everyone is motivated. "Are you saying, Reilly, that everyone in this world is motivated?" the managers challenge in a seminar. Yes!

One sales manager argued, "I have a salesman working for me who shows up late and quits early every day. You're saying this guy is motivated?"

"Sure he is!" I responded. "He's motivated to sleep late and knock off early."

The problem most of us have is that we *assess* versus *accept* another's motivation. This results in our making a value judgment about them.

A young sales manager said about his salesman, "This is the most unmotivated guy I've ever had work for me. When five o'clock hits, he's gone. All he thinks about is coaching his son's soccer team." I understood the salesman to be very motivated. He was motivated to be with his son versus working late. He and his manager may have worked in the same office, but they were worlds apart when it came to their priorities. What really confounded the manager was that the salesman was productive in his job in spite of his being a family man.

People do things for their reasons, not yours. In many cases, they couldn't care less about your reasons. Their behavior is motivated by a unique set of personal needs and values. To influence another's behavior, the most effective strategy is to determine what excites that person and give her the opportunity to experience it as much as possible.

People are motivated to act when these conditions exist:
- She perceives a realistic chance for successfully completing the task.
- The objectives are clear and meaningful.
- The behavior has a valued payoff.
- The person perceives an equity between what she gives and what she gets.
- There is reasonable challenge in the action.

Inducing others to act began when the snake persuaded Eve, and she then tempted Adam to bite the apple. Parents try to motivate children. Coaches whip teams into a frenzied excitement. Managers want employees to achieve maximum productivity.

Each of us, in some fashion, wants to effect some

Simple Psychology

behaviors in other people. The quickest and most effective way to accomplish this is to discover what they want and devise a way to give it to them.

Use it as reinforcement for performing the desired behavior. Make it fun, personalize it, and they'll walk miles for the opportunity to participate.

Today I shall consider another's priorities in my attempts to motivate them.

SECTION TEN

Treat Yourself Right

Do you remember the old jingle, "You deserve a break today . . ."? Well, you do. In fact, you need to *really* treat yourself right. These readings encourage you to celebrate your successes; create good luck; cut yourself some slack; and release your playful inner child.

54: Celebrate Your Successes

"Don't break your arm patting yourself on the back." "Nobody likes a braggart." "Don't flaunt your success." This conventional wisdom, passed down for generations, runs contrary to everyday common sense. Why shouldn't we feel good about our successes?

Are we running so low on our deserve level that we no longer feel good about feeling good? If you've set goals, planned your strategy, worked hard for something and succeeded, you deserve to feel good about your accomplishments. Celebrate your successes, enjoy the feeling, and savor the moment. Feeling good about yourself is one of the most therapeutic things you can do. I'm talking about the healthy self-talk that promotes feelings of worth and esteem, not self-indulgent bragging.

Would you tell a child who just received an "A" on an exam not to feel too good about receiving it? What would you say to an employee who brings you a solution for a problem your company has experienced? "Don't bask in your own glory!" These examples are so ludicrous they barely warrant a footnote in this book. Yet, too many people accept that same bad advice for themselves.

Celebrating your successes has value in two ways. First, there's the emotional aspect. It's self-reinforcing to pat yourself on the back when you do a good job. Feel the excitement. Enjoy being in joy. You deserve it. The positive emotions you feel from this experience provide the start-up fuel you need for your next project. Recording these successes in your own personal victory log provides moments of relief down the road when you may need them.

There's an educational value to your celebrating your successes. Learn from them. Everyone conducts an autopsy on a project that goes badly. "All right, what killed the idea or plan?" Yet, too few conduct a post-event analysis to determine what went right. If you don't know what you're doing right when you're doing it right, how will you know what to do right when you do it wrong? Simple reflection on your success reinforces the principles of success.

At dinner each evening we have a ritual with our children. After our meal prayers I ask them, "What did you do today that you're most proud of?" At first, they didn't know how to respond. They hadn't thought in those terms. After a few evenings they adjusted and came to the table with great anticipation. They could hardly wait to share their delight with the family. I knew this was an important part of their lives but didn't realize just how important until some time later.

I was preoccupied with some issues one evening

and brought them to the table with me. After meal prayers I began eating, not paying much attention to those around me. My daughter said, "Dad, did you forget something?"

Her question caught me off-guard. I looked around the table to make sure I filled my plate with everything my wife prepared. I responded, "No, it looks like I have everything I need."

"Daddy, isn't there something you want to ask us?" Then it hit me, but I played ignorant.

"No, I don't think so," I drawled out.

"What about the question—you know Dad, *the* question?"

"Oh, you mean *the* question?"

"Yeah, Dad, *the* question."

"Well, okay, Amanda, what did you do today that you're really proud of?"

"Wow, Dad, I'm glad you asked." She then elaborated on some event that made her feel great.

It struck me as I listened to Amanda that this was a great forum for positive feedback, recognition, and validation. This was their opportunity to tell those who loved them what a great experience they had and how it made them feel. With each new episode, I could see their confidence growing, self-esteem blooming, and self-image expanding.

It is such an important part of their day that, when I travel and call home at night, they come to the phone to tell me about their day. This part of fatherhood is a thrill to witness: the burgeoning self-worth.

This experience has prompted me to think how the same concept could work for adults. Imagine driving home in the evening and using that forty-five-minute-parking-lot drive as personal time to reflect on what you did that day that makes you proud. Suppose you took this concept a step further and created your own success journal in which you recorded these events and how great they made you feel. You're creating a pattern of success. Underlying this pattern are the dynamics that you wield to your advantage. This success record is your game plan for the future.

You have been given the talent to accomplish great things in this world. Feel passion for your goals. Get excited about your efforts. Be proud of what you are accomplishing. Enjoy your successes. Bathe in the good feelings about yourself. Treat yourself to the same recognition and praise you would give a friend. You would encourage a family member or friend to enjoy their successes, give yourself the same permission. You deserve it.

Today I shall celebrate my successes.

55: Create Your Own Luck

People often say, "I'd rather be lucky than good any day." They presume it's an either/or issue, that you can't be both. I submit that not only can you be both, but it's desirable to be both. Get good and get lucky!

What is luck? Is it coincidence, fate or the divine plan? Maybe, it's a little bit of all three. Most people accept that timing is everything. Some boast, "You can create your own luck." I, too, believe in luck—especially the aggressive kind that you expect and create.

Carl Jung wrote of *coincidental happenings*. His theory states that as you journey through life, many things happen around you. Depending on how you interact with your environment, you are more or less cognizant of these coincidental happenings. As you become aware of them you perceive them as opportunities. Then you're able to take advantage of them. But first they must appear on your radar screen.

I'm a firm believer in the power of expectations. We generally get what we expect in this world, not necessarily what we desire. If you expect coincidental happenings in life, you expand your mental peripheral vision. Your unconscious mental eye scans these events. Because you expect to see them, something activates your intuition and you discover the opportunity.

Dr. Norman Vincent Peale often spoke on the power of positive thinking. He believed in a mental energy that your mind radiates. These signals attract other signals. It's as if our beliefs and expectations draw the consequences we anticipate. I share his belief in positive expectations and energy.

One definition of luck is the point at which preparation meets opportunity. You anticipate an event, prepare yourself to take advantage of it, and begin your mental search for the seeds of this luck. You consciously seek the luck you expect.

So, in a big way you have created your own luck. It begins as hope, grows into expectation and manifests itself as the seed of an opportunity. Those who use this mental peripheral vision expose and exploit the opportunity. Sometimes they're described as having the Midas touch.

One thing you can bet for sure, they were active in

this pursuit. They marshaled their conscious and unconscious resources to expect, recognize and exploit the opportunity. Timing works in their favor but this person doesn't have a monopoly on timing or luck. Luck is democratic. It's evenly and fairly distributed among the population that expects it.

The best way to experience luck is to expect it—energize your unconscious, expand your mental peripheral vision, and seize the opportunity. It's out there for you. Rather than waiting for opportunity to knock on your door, go out there and knock on its door! Be aggressive in your pursuit. The harder you work at it the luckier you'll get.

Today I shall create my own luck.

56: Cut Yourself Some Slack

"Cut me some slack man!" is a familiar plea to give me a break, some room, take it easy on me, or be flexible. What if we enlarged this idea? What if we created a slack factor for ourselves as a living strategy. For example, allow a 10-20% automatic slack factor for the things in your life over which you have little or no control: flight delays, rude waitresses, slow drivers, wrong restaurant orders, or car trouble at the worst possible moment.

These are naturally-occurring events that pester everyone. Do they happen 20% of the time? No. Hopefully not. However, knowing they do occur prepares us for the inevitable waiter who spills our soup or the

Simple Psychology

flight attendant who drops coffee on our manuscripts. It happens. Knowing that it exists in spite of our best efforts offers reassurance that the flow of living contains a little turbulence.

By cutting yourself 10-20% slack each day, you're better prepared to experience these inconveniences. Collectively, I call these slack things—things that naturally occur for which I have very little control. Grant yourself 10-20% leeway to deal with these.

This is not Murphy's Law, it's Reilly's Law—from one Irishman to another. Things happen over which you have little or no control. If you cut yourself 10-20% slack each day to handle slack stuff, you think more clearly during them.

Expect the unexpected. This is not creating negative events in one's life or maintaining a constant vigil for negativity. It's a simple life strategy to help you live through one of life's irritations with minimal inconvenience. The next time you're on a flight and get delayed or sent to the waiting area because your flight arrives early, watch other people around you.

Grown men and women fidget and complain. Some curse the flight attendant, the captain, the FAA, the airport, the airline, and the dog catcher. Others will sit patiently and finish reading their magazines realizing this is slack stuff, and they will cut themselves some slack.

So remember Reilly's Law: stuff happens—it's inevitable—and you'll probably have little or no control over it. For a more peaceful response to help you maintain your sanity, recognize this as slack stuff and give yourself a break—take it easy on yourself. Cut yourself some slack. You'll be glad you did. And so will your

Simple Psychology

blood pressure.

Remember, 10-20% slack per day is a great rule of thumb. On those really good days when you only use half that amount, save the balance in your reserve. And on those 25-30% days, tap into your reserve. You'll always have more than you'll need.

Incidentally, if you haven't guessed by now, I wrote this piece on a delayed flight after an incorrect seat assignment that followed the restaurant's screwing up my lunch order. All-in-all, it's a five percenter!

Today I shall cut myself some slack.

57: Liberate Your Inner Child

Within each of us is a child. Not just the residue of childhood, but a child. The spontaneous, creative, fun-loving, rebellious, immature self that makes life interesting.

Some people repress their inner child. They unconsciously stuff it deep in their psyches rarely to surface or integrate into daily life. These people are born forty years old.

Others consciously suppress their child. They live by the admonition, "Put aside childish things." At some point in their lives they bought into the philosophy that getting older means becoming dull.

Others choose to express the child. They are fun-loving adults that view the rat race as play. They integrate the child into everyday activities. This means they laugh a lot, invent, create, make mistakes, learn, fall down, get back up, make faces at themselves in the mirror, chase butterflies, dream a lot, sing a lot, drink way too much soda, eat too many candy bars, play too many video games, and somehow manage to get the job done.

I submit it's the play that enables them to work so effectively. Play is the primordial sedative. We begin life with a great zest and passion for living. We hate to go to bed at night and can hardly wait to awaken in the morning. Why? Because it's fun! The child is in control of the day—calling the shots.

Freeing the child to enter your life means submitting to your own creativity, spontaneity, and fun-loving activities that make life fun. Integrating the child into your workday adds another dimension of your personality. You find a renewed sense of commitment and pleasure by involving this part of your "sleeping" self.

I've know some brilliant people that should be fascinating to be around, but they're boring. Why? They are too mature. I can't remember seeing them laugh from the pits of their gut. I've known others who were marginally intelligent but were some of the most charismatic people I've met because they laughed at life, at themselves, and could take a joke as much as give one. They're fun!

The message is clear. Lighten up. Have some fun. Let your child express itself. Squeeze the toothpaste from the wrong end of the tube; leave the top off the ketchup bottle; slide down the banister; buy a pack of crayons and draw some clouds; make paper airplanes; cut out paper dolls; and be really silly. Take the child to work with you. Invite him or her to participate in a meeting. Ask for his or her help on a project requiring creativity. Let your child bring the uniqueness that is entirely you. Both of you will be glad you did!

Today I shall liberate my inner child.

SECTION ELEVEN

Get Rid of Useless Emotions

Imagine the life you would live if you purged yourself of the useless emotions that keep you from living a more peaceful and loving life. It's releasing your mental brakes. These readings encourage you to let go of guilt; forgive others; face your fears with courage; stop worrying; and reduce stress.

58: Forgiveness Is Divine

Forgiveness is one of life's greatest challenges. Any serious student of the Bible will tell you that forgiving someone is a prescription for peace and harmony. With that payoff, why is it so difficult?

Is it more natural for us to hold grudges and hate than forgive? Is it because when we forgive, we let the other person off the hook and we're not convinced they deserve it? Failing to forgive may be our way of punishing someone else. It may even feel "good" to get even. You've heard the saying, "Don't get mad, get even."

I watched the Reginald Denny trial segment as he reached over the rail and hugged the family of his alleged attackers. At that moment it occurred to me that maybe this guy, who had such a close brush with death, knew something that could help us.

It's human nature for someone to get angry and maybe hate what another has done. You may be at the point where you don't even want to think the words, "I forgive you." There are phases of forgiveness that begin with anger, grow in compassion, and end with forgiveness. The catharsis of admitting that you're angry with someone is helpful. As there are phases in grieving, you might call this the process of forgiveness. It begins with separating the sin from the sinner and focusing on forgiving the person behind the sin.

There's another aspect of forgiveness. When you forgive someone, there's relief from what you feel. You feel better because you don't carry around the animosity. You've exonerated the other person and liberated yourself. You're no longer a prisoner to your feelings. The forgiveness you offer is as much for you as it is for the other person. When you pray for your enemies, it's difficult to feel hate.

On the other hand, not forgiving empowers the other person to hold something over you long after the event. Why would we give that much power to someone who has treated us badly? It makes more sense to say, "I forgive you and relieve you of your power to hurt me or make me feel bad. I continue to feel bad only if I let myself."

Bitterness. Hatred. Depression. These sound like terrible things to carry around with us. Would you bend over to pick up a bag of bitterness, consume it, and let it feed your hostility? I hope not. Why hang on to bitterness versus forgiving the other person and getting on with life? You can't go through life mad without going mad in the end.

This makes sense on paper but can you live it? Yes. Try. If forgiving someone frees your energy, emotions, and concentration, it's the best thing you can do for yourself. What would you do with all the time you've spent worrying about how to get back at someone you didn't like? If you didn't preoccupy yourself with animosity, how much time could you spend enjoying a sunset, being with your children or playing golf?

Try this for the next thirty days: for better living, try to live life more forgiving.

Today I shall forgive generously.

59: Get Rid Of The Guilts

Is there a more debilitating emotion than guilt? I think not. Remorse, yes. Disappointment, yes. They are more appropriate. But guilt, no.

Some people experience too much while others experience none. A friend of mine said to me one day, "You know what the difference is between you Catholics and us Jews?" At first, I was amazed at his candid and flippant reference to religion.

"No," I said.

"You guys feel guilty for what you *do* and we feel guilty for what we *don't do*." We laughed heartily. No one has a monopoly on guilt.

Neither parents nor children have sole rights to use it. In the process of teaching children right from wrong, parents may cross the line from disappointment with behavior to instill feelings of guilt. Children are vulnerable—they accept the guilt for disappointing their parents. It continues throughout life and in different relationships.

Simple Psychology

At some point, the children may wield their own forms of guilt because they witnessed how effectively their parents manipulated behavior by using it. So they say things like, "You're the worst parent in the world." "You never buy us what we want." "All the other parents let their children watch this program." "You're too tough on me." And if they hit the right theme, Mom or Dad accepts the guilt.

Later in life the parents may return the serve, "You never seem to have much time for Mother and me anymore. I wish we could see the grandchildren more often." And the cycle continues as a tennis game of guilt—serving and receiving.

Children must learn healthy and situationally-appropriate responses. Why inflict guilt when we want to impart accountability for their behavior and appropriate disappointment when they cross the line? Too much turns them neurotic and too little turns them into a menace to society.

As far as the guilt you and I carry around as adults, let's pledge to stop the madness. There must be a better use of your energy than to fret over the beer bottle you threw through a window in college. Since you're playing judge and jury to yourself, give yourself a rational sentence and carry it out. If you carry around some guilt for cheating on your travel expenses, pay for your next trip out of your own pocket.

Your guilt does not change the past: it inhibits your future. Treat yourself as you would a sibling, spouse, or child. Sentence yourself to nothing more than you would them. Experience the disappointment with your behavior. Do the penance, and get on with your life. Let go of what's holding you back.

When dealing with others who sling guilt, consider the source. Remember, you make the decision to accept guilt. If you feel a little sensitive in that area to begin with, you may experience a full-blown guilt attack.

It boils down to two simple questions. "Is guilt really the emotional energy I want my loved ones to experience?" "Do I really want to invest my emotional energy in something as useless as guilt?" If the answer to these questions is a resounding "No," you're on your way to a better life.

***

Today I shall purge myself of guilt.

***

60: Look With Courage Into The Face Of Fear

I grew up on John Wayne and Audie Murphy movies. They made it look so easy—they didn't wince. They had the steadiness of a gunfighter; the selflessness to jump on a grenade to save a buddy; and the guts to stand up to the biggest villain in town. They were bigger-than-life figures that most boys of my time chose as role models. And then we grew up.

This Hollywood image of courage is more glamorous than what I've witnessed in my life. I never saw anyone jump on a grenade in battle, but I saw frightened eighteen-year-old boys fight back tears of terror and hold their position in war. I remember what it felt like the first time someone shot at me. I ducked behind a sandbag wall, and wanted to be at home with mom where everything was safe.

Simple Psychology

I've met terminal cancer patients who were so devastated by their diseases that getting out of bed each morning was an act of courage. I know a woman diagnosed with Multiple Sclerosis who speaks of her condition with optimism and courage. She is a role model to all, and I'm very proud to be her uncle.

I know business people who were so unsettled by the Great Flood of '93 that they barely slept at night but continued to get up every day and go to work to plug it out!

I know several couples who've experienced one of the greatest tragedies of all. They lost a child and managed somehow to pick up the broken pieces and live and love and work another day.

I know several divorced people who made a lifetime commitment to a partner that failed to live up to it. Somehow, the one who's been hurt makes it.

I've seen courage in young people who lost their parents early or never even knew them. Somehow, they persisted.

Courage isn't anything like Hollywood. Courage and fear have much in common. They generally occur together. The most courageous people I know are also some of the most scared people I know. It's unrealistic to believe that courage stamps out fear.

When I was stationed at Ft. Leonard Wood, on my way to Vietnam, they impressed upon us this message: courage is not the absence of fear, it's the management of fear. You're courageous when you are afraid and still do what you must do. Feel the fear and act.

Courage is positive behavior in the midst of fear. Physically, your body is up to the challenge because of the autonomic nervous system's *fight or flight* reaction.

Simple Psychology

Like all animals, humans are genetically encoded to deal with threatening situations. Mentally, it's another story. The decision is based on reason and emotion. Sometimes emotion wins, other times reason wins.

In every courageous act is a lot of fear. Within courageous people is an equally powerful desire to flee the situation. Courageous people are not immune from fear. It's just as vivid for them: maybe more so. The only difference is that they act in spite of their fear.

The courageous people who fight life's everyday battles share a common denominator with their ancestral warriors. They, too, feel the fear. They are overwhelmed by an illness and muster the courage to persevere. They are knocked down by a business or personal failure and somehow find the courage to rise from it. They suffer a devastating loss in life and, at the point of no return, discover the hidden pocket of strength that fuels them for another day.

These are our contemporary heroes. These are courageous men, women, and children who experience the fear and persevere. They take the full brunt of what life hands them; and in spite of their worries and fears, tap into the indefatigable human spirit to hang in there for one more day. They refuse to quit.

And you, my friend, are one of these people. Within you is a vast reservoir of strength and courage to use during times of great tribulation. Will you be scared? Possibly. Will you want to flee? Yes, probably. Will you feel the fear and do the right thing? I'm betting you will.

Today I shall face life with courage.

61: On Being Judgmental

When my children were younger, we sat in the cry room at church. Cry-room parents develop a camaraderie with their peers. They're experiencing similar things at the same point in their lives. Even though you may not know another couple well, you develop an affinity for them because of your common situation. There was a couple with two children about the ages of ours. We saw them over several weeks, and we were in the pleasant nodding phase with them.

One Sunday their little one was particularly active doing the things two-year-olds do. He was busy. The father reached the point of no return and grabbed the child harshly, shook him, and spanked him on the bottom. I felt badly for them. I thought the father overreacted. And it bothered me enough that was it difficult to be cordial to him after mass.

Later, in the car I said to my wife, "Don't you think he overreacted and took it out on the kid."

With boundless wisdom, my wife said, "It's a tough call to judge him. You don't know what happened before Mass and what kind of morning they had with the child. Besides, where's your patience?"

She was right. I was judging without walking a mile in his shoes. The bittersweet irony is that I was doing this in church notwithstanding the Christian mandate of "Judge not, lest you be judged." In fact, all great religions and spiritual thinkers admonish us not to judge our neighbors. Common sense tells us that judging is a poor use of our time.

People often employ the defense mechanism, projection. It's attributing our thoughts and feelings to others because it's easier to recognize our faults in someone else than ourselves. So, the next time you hear someone say, "Boy, ol' Frank is about the most two-faced individual I've ever met," the person is probably talking about himself—projection.

Why do people judge? It's a leveling technique. If I feel inferior to someone, the quickest way to level the playing field is to denigrate that individual. Because they're diminished, in a twisted way I feel stronger. It's building oneself up by breaking others down. This is a weak foundation for building self-esteem. To be strong only because another is weak is not very personally enhancing.

There's an inverse relationship between judging others and how we feel about ourselves. The worse we feel about ourselves, the more we judge those around us. Many walk with an air of superiority on the outside because of the inferiority they feel on the inside. They mask their feelings of insecurity behind a facade of confidence. In many cases it's obvious to everyone except them.

When I'm with someone who judges another, I hear the inner voice of the critic deep inside him, and I pity his insecurity. It's one thing to criticize a behavior and another to denigrate the person doing the behavior. When I feel myself being judgmental, I remind myself of the passage from the poem, **Desiderata**:

"If you compare yourself with others, you may become vain or bitter, for always there will be greater and lesser persons than you."

Today I shall avoid judging others.

62: Stop Worrying And Start Living

Worry is a first-class waste of time and energy. And yet we do so much of it. We have been taught not to worry, but we do it anyway. Parents, teachers, mentors, and even the Bible tell us not to worry: "Have no anxiety about anything, but in everything by prayer and supplication, with thanksgiving, let your requests be made known to God." (Philippians 4:6) "Be strong and of good courage; be not frightened, neither be dismayed; for the Lord your God is with you wherever you go." (Joshua 1:9)

We worry about financial issues, grades, making the big sale, and impressing people. We preoccupy ourselves with self-doubt and undeserved criticism. We spend valuable time fretting over our health and physiques. Will I impress my new boss? What will the minister think of my divorce? Will my family like my new girlfriend? Will I be accepted by my first-choice college?

Legitimate concern stops short of unnecessary worry. Without a phone call, your teenager stays out two hours beyond curfew. How you process that determines whether it's legitimate concern or excessive worry. Worrying behavior is the hand wringing, feeling helpless, I'm-a-victim reaction. Legitimate concern is, "I'm going to make a few phone calls to find out what happened. I'm uneasy but still in control of my emotions." The difference is how you choose to process it.

You can replace worry with positive action. This doesn't negate the anxiety. It offers an alternative expression. When you worry about your health, get a check-up to alleviate your concerns. Follow up with an exercise program and better diet. Instead of worrying about retirement funds, curtail spending; get a good financial planner; work a little overtime; and begin a savings plan. Instead of moping around because your latest love rejected you, go to dances and meet someone new. If you're preoccupied about getting into the right school, spend time preparing for the entrance exam. If you're concerned about being laid off, invest in your performance. Use the worrying energy as working energy.

This is not denial. You will feel appropriate uneasiness. Otherwise, it means you really don't care. The trick is to replace unnecessary and useless worrying behavior with positive action that moves you closer to your goals. Replace fear with hope, and focus on what you want to happen, not what you want to avoid.

It's a pitiful life when you live it by worrying about the things you want to avoid versus things you want to experience. How you choose to use your mental energy determines behavior. It's hard to worry when you're investing your time in positive ways. Spiritual fuel helps also. Find a scripture that gives you strength and repeat it often during your times of worry. You need not do this alone.

Today I shall eliminate worry from my mind.

63: Stressless Living

Having lived through my share of stressful life events (war, cancer, deaths of both parents, floods, two business start-ups, etc.), I felt qualified when a customer asked me to speak to his sales group on stress. In a smug sort of way I thought, "Boy, can I teach these guys something about how to deal with stress." I made two important discoveries. First, regardless of who you are and what you've experienced, the truth is *stress hurts*. Second, if you want to have someone speak to your group on stress, hire an expert who understands the medical implications. As I researched the topic, I discovered how much I didn't know about stress.

For example, did you know that stress is a choice we make? As things happen around us, we input these experiences, process them and make decisions (based on our perceptions an beliefs) how we want to react. This explains why some people perceive an event as stress and others view it as challenge. It has plenty to do with one's belief about the event. Asking oneself a question before reacting can make a huge difference in one's perception: "Is there another way to view this?" This challenges you to be aware of other possible interpretations which can lead to different responses.

If someone cuts you off in traffic, how do you react? Angry? Make an obscene gesture? Speed up to retaliate? Is there another possibility? Could that person be on the way to the hospital for an emergency? One choice brings stress and the other brings empathy. Give the other person (and yourself) the benefit of the doubt?

Something else I discovered is that we stress ourselves, especially when we are not in control. "How much control do I have over this situation?" If the answer is a lot, change the situation. If the answer is not very much, you either roll with the waves or avoid the situation.

Denying stress doesn't work either. A friend of mine said to me one day in his most macho tone, "I do stress for a living." Unless you're an adrenaline junkie, don't! My suspicion is that my friend will someday feel the full brunt of his denial. Then, it might be too late to do anything about it.

Most stress is self-inflicted. Expectations energize or pressurize. Unrealistically high expectations create stress. Deadlines kill. Why do they call them deadlines? Sure, you need target dates to avoid procrastination. The key is to create realistic expectations that motivate, not frustrate.

At times, we create such a flurry of activity that nothing important happens, but we're very busy being very busy. Over-achievers create a lot of their own headaches by attempting way too much in too short a time period. Generally, your body lets you know when you're attempting too much. Listen to it. It knows what's best for you.

I've created for myself a list of *Stress-firmations*. I review these each week to be proactive in dealing with my self-imposed stress.

- To reduce stress, I must do more of less.
- I upset myself when I feel stress.
- I control my emotional response with self-talk.
- Do I want to invest valuable energy on this?

I also use interrupt strategies to break the cycle of anxiety: take a walk; listen to a tape; fly a kite; read the Bible; or breathe from the diaphragm: nose in, hold for ten, breathe out through the mouth. Stress does not need to kill you. It can be a positive energy source if you choose to use it that way. It depends on how you process it.

Maximize your positive control. Set realistic target dates. Drink less caffeine. Have a physical outlet to vent steam. Don't waste a hundred dollars worth of energy on a nickel-and-dime problem. Stress is mostly a do-it-to-yourself disease. So is the solution. Learn from your stress. In the words of St. Bernard:

"Nothing can work me damage except myself; the harm that I sustain, I carry about with me, and never am I a real sufferer but by my own fault."

Today I shall free myself from stress.

SECTION TWELVE

You're Very Special

Look at your fingertips. Each is decorated with an imprint of your uniqueness. You are definitely a one-of-a-kind person! These readings reinforce the importance of this message. You're very special and deserve special recognition. Read and enjoy this celebration of what your Creator intended you to be: you.

64: It's Okay To Be Different!

From our earliest days society has molded us. The socialization process fills our need to belong. We spend much of our lives getting to know the right people, going to the right schools, belonging to the right clubs, wearing the right clothes, playing the right sports, living in the right neighborhood, worshipping at the right church, donating to the right charities, banking at the right bank, eating the right foods at the right restaurants, driving the right car, shopping at the right stores, vacationing at the right places, working for the right company, advocating the right causes, seeing the right movies, and projecting the right attitude.

We do this to fit in somewhere—the right place. We stifle that which is special. It's a wonder why we don't go out of our minds. In the process, we forget that we're blessed with a set of unique fingerprints. It's God's way of saying, "It's okay to be different!" There's a biblical mandate to express this. "Do not neglect the gift that is in you." (1 Timothy 4:14)

Unless we permit ourselves to be different, how can we express our unique talents or gifts bestowed on us by our Creator? He knew what He was doing when He gave us these unique gifts.

It's difficult to break loose from a lifetime of conventional behavior. I'm not referring to those who go out of their way to be different. I believe their motive is to be contrary—thumbing their collective noses at society. What I'm describing is the independent personality that allows for uniqueness and idiosyncrasies to enter into daily living.

Weave your unique flair into daily habits. There is something very special about your interpretation of who you are. Attempting to fit in all the time inhibits this.

Do something unusual and weird. Write with a purple marker. Take a nap at noon. Sleep at the foot of the bed. Eat pizza for breakfast. Make love in a field of flowers. And if this unconventional behavior pushes the limits of your comfort zone, do what I do. I'm one of the few business people in St. Louis who rides to work on a Harley, briefcase hanging from the back.

Stoke the coals of uniqueness deep within you. There's a unique passion smoldering in your spirit. Fan the coals of individuality. Let them rage like a blast furnace of independence. It's okay to be different. In fact, you owe it to yourself. It is the ultimate right thing to do.

Today I shall assert my uniqueness.

65: Soar With Your Strengths

Each of us is able to perform some task better than 99.9% of the population. Whether it's singing a song, driving a golf ball, painting a portrait, skiing a mountain, or writing a novel, each of us possesses an excellence, a special talent or strength, that sets us apart.

Concentrating your strengths in a focused area enables you to go for real depth. When you compete in a generalized sense, you're battling with the top 10-20% in each field of people who specialize in using their special talent.

Everyday I work with groups of salespeople and managers who keep their talents hidden or partially buried. Many people underestimate their potential and never fully exercise their talent. It's sad that they may never really discover what's inside them. They settle for second best and fail to use the rest.

Each of us is so uniquely talented that when we pursue our special gift we experience little competition.

Emerson wrote...

"Each man has his own vocation. The talent is the call. There is one direction in which all space is open to endless exertion. He inclines to do something which is easy to him, and good when it is done, but which no other man can do. He has no rival."

When you discover your proficiencies, and concentrate your efforts with a laser-beam intensity in that area, you enjoy a much higher return on your time and effort invested.

The first step is to determine your strengths or unique talents. Which is more natural for you, arts or science? Are you more comfortable with philosophy or numbers? Do you prefer to work with your mind or body? What do you have a special knack for doing? Can you tell a good story? Does technology fascinate you? Are you musically inclined? Would you rather have a job that involved being around people or do you prefer to work independently? Are you mechanically inclined? Are there things you so passionately enjoy that you do them even though you don't get paid? What things seem effortless and when you do them you feel alive and at your personal best? When do people compliment your performance?

These penetrating, insightful questions will help you identify your strengths and your preferences. Once you've identified these areas place yourself in situations where you have an opportunity to fully exploit these talents.

What about your weaknesses? Will you ever be able to take a weakness and make it a strength? The odds are not in your favor. On the other hand, you can minimize the effect of your weaknesses. For example, if personal organization is not a strength, purchase and use one of the great time management systems on the market. The Franklin Planner is a great tool to use to keep you organized. You probably won't become a time management expert, but you may learn to manage the problem in a way so that it doesn't limit you.

Many people go through life a mile-wide and an inch-deep. They're way too shallow. They fail to develop fully their unique talent. Others go through life an inch-wide and a mile-deep. They develop fully and use their unique gift. They understand that you need to exercise your strengths and talents to get full utilization. Let them out. Use them. Develop them.

Thomas Wolfe wrote:

"If a man has a talent and doesn't use it, he has failed. If he has a talent and uses part of it, he has partly failed. But if he has a talent and somehow manages to use the whole of it, he has gloriously succeeded and won a satisfaction and triumph few men and women will ever know."

You have the talent. You have the opportunity. The rest is up to you.

Today I shall soar with my strengths.

66: Enjoy The Richness Of Your Personality

Within you is a rich and rare collection of life experiences. The more you experience life and integrate it into your personality, the more alive you become. Your personality is a dynamic force within you—growing, emerging, and evolving. You feed it and fuel it with life.

You feel alive when you allow the different aspects of your personality to express themselves: creativity, joy, disappointment, sadness, stress and freedom. These are the emotions and the states of the mind. Who feels life more than someone who is deeply saddened by the death of a loved one? Who does life affect more than the person elevated by the birth of a child?

As you experience all that life offers—pain and pleasure—and internalize the experience, your ever-changing dynamic self emerges, better for the experience. As debilitating as stress can be, there is an accompanying perk. As you respond to tough situations, you develop an inner strength. These coping mechanisms are available for the future. They rest in your vast reservoir of life experiences. Faith and hope have played a major role in the development of personality.

As you allow for the full expression of love in your life, you open yourself to the wonderful bonds between people. It's impossible to be unaffected by this. As you love and are loved, you accept part of that person into your being and give part of you to them. You change each other.

Living life. Feeling life. Loving life. This is the magical ability humans have over animals. Weaving these life experiences into your being creates the integrated self—a fully feeling, alive individual. Imagine how much richer your life can be if you view your every waking hour as part of the growth process. You're constantly becoming more of you.

The logic follows that your brightest days are in the future. As good as today feels, tomorrow will be better. Your prescription for growth is to:

- Grow spiritually—spend time daily with your Creator. Ask your Creator to share, as a partner, in your successes and failures.
- Develop yourself intellectually. Mind stretching builds your acquired ability.
- Tap into your creative self. Do something that allows your creative side to emerge.
- Love a lot. Heal yourself and others with this biblical elixir.
- Feel the setbacks in life. They, too, mean you're alive and vibrant.

Within you is your integrated self. It's a mosaic of

life experiences that define only you. Others may share your genetic make-up and some of your experiences, but only you can produce the life that is uniquely you. You and your life are special creations. Inseparable. Enjoy this. Your Creator planned it that way.

Today I shall enjoy and express the richness of my personality.

67: Self Actualization: Your Best You!

Over fifty years ago, Abraham Maslow introduced the concept of self-actualization and spawned generations of believers in a psychology of personal growth/development. His need-satisfaction theory of motivation is a staple in introductory psychology courses and management seminars.

Maslow proposed a hierarchy of needs beginning with the most basic and ranked in ascending order of importance. At the bottom of this hierarchy are biological needs: the need for water, food, air, sex, etc. Once that level of need is satisfied we are motivated to satisfy the next higher level of need: security needs. And once that level is satisfied we are drawn to the next higher level, love and belongingness. Then, we are drawn to satisfy the next higher level need, esteem. And so it goes until we reach the peak experience of self-actualization.

This is a satisfaction-progression model because we progress to the next higher level of needs as a lower level is satisfied. Once a need is satisfied it no longer carries the same motivational impact. That's why we're drawn to the next higher level. This explains why people whose money needs are met are not as motivated by money. They're satisfied.

Lower-level needs are satisfied externally: food, air, sex, shelter, pay, work conditions, recognition, acceptance by a reference group, etc. Upper-level needs for autonomy, challenge, creative expression, esteem, and becoming everything you can become (self-actualization) are satisfied internally.

It's an easy model to teach managers for use in job design. When managers create environments that give employees the opportunity to satisfy many of these levels of needs on the job, they create more highly motivated workers.

This model is a straightforward way to describe what moves people. This is applied psychology at its best.

Maslow was encouraging a psychology of hope. If self-actualization is the state of "becoming all that one can become," and is the only level of need that is never fully satisfied, the logic follows: humans are aspiring, evolving, and emerging organisms. We are in a constant state of getting better: we are growth-oriented.

Common-sense tells us that each of us wants to be better today than yesterday, and better tomorrow than today. How many people awaken in the morning, look in the mirror and say, "Yeah, today I'm going out there and be mediocre. And when it comes to being average I'm the best"? It doesn't work that way. We are evolving, growth-oriented organisms that operate best when we drive in our forward gear. Maslow was right.

Simple Psychology

We have different levels of needs, and at any given time one is more prepotent than the others. But the most influential of all is the need to find out how much we have inside of us: the need to grow to our full potential. No other animal on this earth makes conscious decisions to actualize. Humans alone possess that power. You create your best you. This restless curiosity is a powerful motivator.

Today I shall become the best within me.

68: Self Identity

The next time you board an airplane, observe how long it takes for the person next to you to ask, "Who are you with or what type of work do you do?" Is this casual small talk or is our identity determined by what we do, for whom we work, or our relationship to another person?

Who we are is different from *what we are*; further from *what we do*; and more distant from what we own. Each of us has a unique set of fingerprints. We are defined by this uniqueness: the values that we hold dear, our morality, and the image of our Creator. We're more than our collective life experiences or what we've collected in a lifetime. Our self-identity is the dynamic concept of who we are becoming.

I wonder how many people give themselves permission to become more of what they're capable of becoming. I pity those who fail to look inward for a uniquely personal description of their identity. What happens

Simple Psychology

when they stop being vice president, athlete, speaker, mom, dad, brother, wife, husband, son, or daughter?

If their identity comes from the outside, they're unsure of who they are. Imagine waking up at age sixty-two, your children are raised, your spouse has died, and you've just been laid off from your job. If your identity comes from external things, you're lost. How many people in their forties run off to find themselves because time is slipping away and they desperately need an identity for the rest of it?

You don't need to join a commune, spend years in therapy, or practice an eastern religion to find the answer. Just ask yourself a few questions. For example, "Beyond what I own and do for a living, who am I? Aside from those around me, how would I describe myself? What do I really believe in? What would I die for? If I were left alone tomorrow, who would I really be?"

Emerson's essay, <u>Self-Reliance</u>, provides us with an eloquent backdrop as we journey inward . . .

"Men have looked away from themselves and at things so long that they have come to...measure their esteem of each other by what each has and not by what each is...nothing can bring you peace but yourself."

Emerson wrote prolifically on the relationship between man and his Creator. He understood that when humans question their being, never are they closer to their Maker or the answer to the question, "Who am I?"

Today I shall journey inward.

SECTION THIRTEEN

Time

The promise of technology is more time. The reality of technology is that we've discovered ways to do more and more in less and less time. This creates an even greater urgency for managing one's time better. This goes on and on and on. It's enough to wear you out! The readings in this section are written to help you adjust your attitude toward time and to get more important things done in the time you have available. You have a choice over how you invest your life and this section will help you clarify those choices.

69: Gifts Of Time

An immutable fact of nature is that time is our most precious and democratic resource. Everyone has the same twenty-four hours per day, seven days per week, three hundred and sixty-five days every year. Some view it as a commodity: they spend it, save it, waste it, trade it, and kill it. How often have you heard, "I just wish I had more time," or "I'm out of time," or "There aren't enough hours in the day to do the things I want to do"?

Time management is a misnomer. We manage ourselves, not time. Managing ourselves means understanding that we invest our time in ways that provide us with the outcomes we desire from life.

Everyday life blesses us with *gifts of time*, the

Simple Psychology

twenty-minute wait at the doctor's office; the five-minute wait in a grocery store line; the two-hour delay at airports between flights; the thirty-minute holding pattern before landing; the extra commute time during an especially tough rush hour; the seasonally slow service at malls; the customer who keeps a salesperson waiting for twenty minutes; the extra fifteen minutes we spend watching movie screens before the feature starts; the time we "kill" waiting for busses or car pool rides; the time between classes, and the list goes on.

Everyday living treats us to these moments of life, these *gifts of time*. Some people view them as aggravations, irritations or time wasters. Others see them as blessings. Your attitude toward these *gifts of time* determines your stress level. Once I accepted the inevitability of the *gifts of time*, my attitude changed. They became opportunities, not irritants.

Of course, I had some prompting. I vividly recall lying in the intensive care unit at Memorial City Hospital in Houston wondering if I would live or die from the cancer they discovered in my body. I was in serious condition. The surgery lasted several hours and involved a great deal of tissue removal from my throat and neck. The doctor couldn't guess what might happen next. It was wait and see.

I was lying in the bed wishing that I were a few hundred feet away stuck in the slow-moving, rush-hour traffic on the Katy freeway. Anyone who has ever experienced that traffic jam would question my sanity at that moment. I suddenly craved the boredom of daily living: long, slow-moving lines; sunsets and sunrises; screaming children in church; long waits in restaurants; and the beautiful frustration of being delayed by the foursome in front of me on the golf course! Life was slipping away and I desperately wanted to feel every moment.

Today, sixteen years later, I still think about the boredom of daily living. Sometimes I stress myself when I must wait, but it's generally a self-inflicted wound. Then I remember I'm blessed with a *gift of time* and treat myself to a special use of these moments. I'm more cognizant now of how I use this gift. I'm more proactive these days. When I'm prepared for them, I lower my stress.

I travel these days in walking shoes. Excessive delays between flights are opportunities to get some bonus exercise at the airport. Holding patterns on planes give me an opportunity to finish reading the novel I've been carrying for weeks.

Long rush-hour lines are really two *gifts of time*. On the one hand, I mercifully watch the angry faces of other drivers and feel for them. They are stressed and hate what they're experiencing. Their frustration is a constant reminder of these *gifts of time*. I use this time to listen to music. I may use this time to dictate a letter or an article. Or, I may just sit there and drink in the relaxing music as a great buffer between the pressures of the day and the time I want to spend with my family that night.

Grocery store lines these days are opportunities to spend time with my Creator—a few minutes of silent reflection on the many blessings He gives me. If I stand in a slow-moving line for an amusement ride or movie, I may enjoy the anticipation or use it as an opportunity to meet a new friend.

Do I still get frustrated by these things? Sure. It

generally happens when I over schedule and under prepare. My expectations have a lot to do with the stress I feel.

I try to maximize the *gifts of time* and minimize the irritations. It's not only possible—it's preferable. Treat yourself to the *gifts of time* attitude: you'll be glad you did!

Today I shall treat myself to gifts of time.

70: Time Management Is Really Self-Management

Time. Everyone wants more. For some people, it's a competitive advantage. For others, it's a disaster. Some view it as a stressor because they don't have enough. Others look for ways to kill time because they have too much. Children can't wait for it to pass more quickly. Older folks wish it would slow down. Some folks would like to turn back the hands of time while others would enjoy jumping forward.

Dealing more effectively with time begins with accepting a few realities about it. First, good time management begins with a fundamental respect for everyone's time. When you respect your time, you find it easier to say "No" to interruptions and time wasters. If you do not respect your time, no one else will respect it. When other people see how much you value time, they avoid wasting it. This also means you don't waste others' time. The value of your time does not make their time less valuable. If you want respect, you give respect.

Second, accept that life is unfinished. When you die, you will leave some things undone. There will be books you wanted to read; places you wanted to visit; and stuff you wanted to do. Life ends untidy. Once you accept that, it's easier to leave the office at night with a few things undone on your daily list. You feel less guilty for the things you failed to do. You focus on doing that which is most important. If everything cannot get done, you must do the high-priority things that help you achieve your goals.

Third, of all the success dynamics—education, background, family—the most democratic is time. Everyone has the same amount of it. Why do some people accomplish more of what they want than others? It has everything to do with the choices they make about their time. How do you choose to use your time? Do you invest it in those areas that will give you the return that you want, or waste it in low-payoff areas?

Fourth, you can either work hard or work smart. Hard work is admirable but not enough. A friend of mine is fond of saying, "The nose-to-the-grind-stone and shoulder-to-the-wheel philosophy of life leads to bloody noses and tired shoulders." Smart work is knowing what to do and what not to do. It's easy to figure out which projects to work on but difficult to know which projects not to work on.

Fifth, fill your days and weeks with high-payoff activities. Begin your day with the question, "What do I want to accomplish vs. what do I need to get done?" It's more than a semantic difference: it's attitudinal. The first question is proactive and the second is reactive. With the first, you attack your day. With the second, your day attacks you. Who's running whom? Are you calling the shots? Or, is your day running you? Do you run your business or does your business run you?

So, we're really back to where we started. Good time management is good self-management. Manage yourself and you'll manage your time.

Today I shall become a better self-manager.

71: Choose Your Day

After the Great Flood of '93 friends called to determine how badly we got hit and how we were doing. One friend called several times to check on me. He was convinced I should be depressed. And if he couldn't find it, I was denying it.

"Tom, how are you today?" Jack asked.

"Fine," I replied.

"You say that, but how are you really feeling?"

"I'm *really* feeling okay."

"You know, this depression stuff is pretty serious and can do some weird things to your mind," my concerned friend said.

"Well, since I'm weird to begin with, it may not affect me as much as other people." We laughed.

Jack wasn't the only one to ask about my mental health. I guess others really felt that if there was a problem, that's where it first shows up.

After several concerned individuals persisted, I developed a standard response to their question. "You know, this flood business is pretty much like life in general except more so. I wake up in the morning and decide what type of day I want to have and then go about creating it. If I want a really crummy day, I think about not having insurance; losing some equipment; having my new building, of which I was so proud, devastated to the tune of $100,000; and working from my home. Pretty depressing stuff isn't it?

"Or, if I wake up in the morning and decide that today I want to have a great day, I think about the ninety-five percent of the equipment we evacuated; the following Monday we were open for business; on Tuesday, we shipped $8,000 worth of books, and that my business was up 35% over the previous year—our best year ever! We have our health. We have our friends. We have our house. We have an incredible amount of love and support. We're doing great!"

Was I stressed? You bet. Was I disappointed? Of course. Did I feel some insecurity? Sure. I felt all that and more! They were situationally appropriate. But I had a choice for the type of day I wanted to live. It began in my mind and I lived it in the flesh.

What type of day do you want to have today? What type of commute do you want to have to the office today? What type of relationship do you want to have with your spouse and children? How do you want to fill your day and live your life—in the avoidance of pain or the pursuit of gain? Will you have a crummy or great day? Once you make the decision of what kind of day you want to have and begin to look in that direction, be careful—you may get what you want!

Today I shall create and live the type of day I desire.

72: Procrastination

This is the habit of putting off until tomorrow that which we could do, and most likely should do, today. Procrastination is avoidance behavior. You do it to avoid something: pain, boredom, fear, etc.

If you want to determine why you procrastinate ask, "What do I avoid by delaying this?" The avoidance is your payoff.

One man's pain is another man's pleasure. Last summer my son, Paul, decided to cut the grass to avoid cleaning the garage—he hates the job. Funny. I cleaned the garage to avoid cutting the grass. I hate that job.

We put off the unpleasant, painful, and boring: work projects, decisions, paperwork, trips to the dentist, diets, drawing up wills, and asking the boss for a raise. Each represents a potentially unpleasant thing to do. So, we avoid the pain by putting them off to another day. I wonder if we secretly hope the situation will go away or somehow remedy itself.

The chronic procrastinator (the Scarlet O'Hara Syndrome) is the person who lives the lifestyle of perpetually putting most things off. This person has great difficulty accomplishing very much.

The prescription for everyday procrastination is action. Get busy doing something. Action is the link between desire and achievement. Action will help you crack the inertia. Ask yourself this question, "Is it worth the aggravation and the persistent nagging feeling—especially if I'll have to do it anyway?" If putting off something means you'll sit around and think about doing it while not doing it, why wait?

Do you really want to use valuable energy in a totally unrewarding manner? It won't be any easier to do it later than it is to do it now. And you may discover that doing it isn't as bad as you thought it would be. That would be a great surprise!

The remedy is action. Break the inertia. Segment the task into small, meaningful units and execute the first step. You'll surprise yourself at how easy it is to continue. It's rarely as bad as you anticipate.

At this moment think of something you have been putting off. What is it? What are you avoiding by not doing it? Is it worth the aggravation of delay? Will you still need to do it after procrastinating? Do you preoccupy yourself with it even though you're not acting on it? What's the first small step you can take to crack the inertia? Get busy.

I'd love to spend more time on this topic but there's a dental appointment I need to make.

Today I shall accomplish one thing I've procrastinated.

SECTION FOURTEEN

Your Relationship With Others

Each of us is an important part of something much bigger than ourselves. We live in a world where interdependence is critical for our survival. The readings in this section offer you ideas on how to interact with others in your environment. They encourage you to look for the good in others; respect fellow humans; deal effectively and compassionately with tough people; and be aware of the lessons others teach us.

73: Seeing Christ In Everyone

A few nights ago my wife and I were out with friends. At dinner, we discussed various things, and our friend, Mary Lou, told us that she loved people so much that she could see Christ in everyone. I thought this was something nice to feel and say. And if you knew her, you would believe that she feels this way. She loves people.

Her comment entered my mental incubator and cooked for a few days. Then I began to think about it on a more conscious level. This is a woman whom people dearly love. She has more friends than any one person I know. She's positive to be around and a loving mother and wife. And she's an incredibly normal, down-to-earth person. She smokes an occasional cigarette, has a glass of wine with dinner, and may raise her voice when dealing with her children. The all-American mom.

How does someone develop this attitude? She looks for and finds Christ in everyone. She begins with the premise that it's there and looks for it. Her philosophy is simple. "It's there along with some other things I'll find. I will look beyond the warts."

What a great philosophy! Looking for Christ in all people is a very positive way of looking for the best in others. And you don't need to be a Christian to live this principle. It means looking for the good in others: the love, the kindness, and the talents—supremely positive attributes. Looking and loving.

What would it mean if we all believed and practiced this? How many people could we influence positively if we accepted another's imperfections as only a part of the total package for being supremely human? Maybe there would be fewer divorces; less need to argue with other people; and more genuine love in the world. I believe it would happen.

So, I too will be looking for Christ in everyone I meet. I know it's there. Maybe on some days I'll need to work a little harder at it. And I'm certain that with some people I will need to search a little longer to find it. But, I know that it's a much better use of my energy than focusing on their negative attributes.

Mary Lou's idea has had real staying power. Her words are still ringing in my mind's ear. Maybe a good place to start is at home, at work, at church, or at the grocery store.

If I invest my time in looking for the good in others, I won't have the time, energy, or inclination to look for the other things that give me stress or make me feel superior in some way. I won't have the time to judge others. I'll be too busy looking for the thing that makes them special. And if I find it, I wonder what will come out of me as a reflection of their goodness? Thanks, Mary Lou.

Today I shall look for Christ in everyone I meet.

74: Respect

Parents and teachers talk about it. Aretha Franklin sings about it. Rodney Dangerfield never gets it. And in a twisted sort of way, gang members make it part of their street code. It's the one thing the world needs more of—a simple virtue.

Respect for self. It's how we esteem ourselves, the regard we hold for us, and the consideration we direct inward. It's fundamental to our treating our bodies, minds, and souls in ways that benefit us. We want it from ourselves and others and give it to get it.

How can we reasonably expect others to respect us if we don't respect ourselves? It begins with how we let others treat us. We must believe that we are worthy of respect. We are. Everyone needs it and deserves it. How we project respect for ourselves determines how others treat us. Start with the belief that you deserve it. You are an important person. Within you is a greatness and uniqueness that only you bring to this world.

Respect for God. Our Creator is the center of the universe. It is because of Him that all of us exist. The old saying "God-fearing" was a way to admonish the importance of showing reverence to God. Many argue that respect for anything begins with a respect for God.

Respect for your country. It's important to respect your country. Respect doesn't mean making it better by destroying it. It also doesn't mean blindly following your politicians when they are wrong. Respecting your country is working within the system to change what needs fixing. It is serving not just extracting. It's paying your full due even when it comes to taxes. It's standing at and observing our National Anthem. On Memorial Day, watch a veteran attending a service for fallen comrades. When they play the National Anthem, he'll have a tear in his eye for the respect he feels.

Respect for others. Just as we deserve it, so do others. Respecting yourself does not give you the right to disrespect other people. Something we hear too little of today is respect for elders. When I grew up this was a basic value taught by our parents. I think my generation needs to work harder on passing the legacy on to our children. This includes respect for teachers, police, clergy, neighbors, bosses, and employees.

Respecting another means we accept that they have a right to express their opinions. They have a right to their own property—it's not ours to take. They have a right to express their uniqueness in lawful ways. They have a right to participate in the American Dream. This is taught in the homes first and reinforced in the churches and schools. Perhaps we need a curriculum of respect.

Imagine a world where everyone accepted the rights of others and respected them. There would be less crime on the streets, less abuse in the homes, more genuine learning in the schools, and better governing in our capitol. Respect is an amazingly simple virtue—maybe the simplest of all.

Simple Psychology

Today I shall give respect freely.

75: Handling Difficult People

There are some people in this world who are just plain tough to deal with. They get along with no one. They're obstinate, contrary, and miserable to be around. They don't appear to like other people and may not care much about themselves. They may perceive relationships as too much work; they may not trust other people; and their negativity speaks volumes about what is going on in their heads.

When I meet someone like this I'm generally struck by their paradoxical behavior. The thing they need most from life is what they appear to guard against—love and acceptance from others. Some of these folks work very hard at not being accepted by others. And yet, belonging is what they crave. I assume they lack the social skills to pull it off. They don't know how to get close to people.

Should you lend a helping hand? Some might argue that if you extend a helping hand to feed a hungry dog, the dog may bite the hand that feeds it. Others may argue that the dog may lick the hand that feeds it. So what's the answer?

Spiritually-inclined people might risk the bite to feed the hungry. Streetwise, fool-me-once, shame-on-you, fool-me-twice, shame-on-me people may be less willing to take the risk. And that's what relationships require— risk.

In loving, we risk rejection. In helping, we risk being told to butt out. In feeding, we risk being bitten. The person who wears a tough facade could be defending against feelings of insecurity and fears rejection. Beneath this difficult exterior may be a scared little boy or girl attempting to make it in this world.

These ideas may help you navigate your way through some turbulent relationships. First, their negativity, contrariness, and toughness must not define your response. That's something you decide. Do not allow yourself to get drawn into their game. And that's what it is. It's a coping mechanism they learned somewhere along the way.

Second, don't take their behavior personally. This person has not singled you out of the crowd and decided to treat you this way. He probably treats everyone this way. This says more about him than you.

Third, give yourself time to respond. Use patient listening. Try to understand the emotion the other person is expressing. Empathy is a great predecessor to expression. If you can feel what this person feels and express your understanding, you've dismantled one of the barriers this person has built.

Fourth, separate the behavior from the person. This may be difficult because it appears endemic to his personality. Although you may find the behavior obnoxious and difficult to be around, can you find a little light in this person? Is there a way for you to help this little light shine? Finding this little light may be the only kindness this person has experienced in a long time.

To some, these ideas may be more trouble than they're worth. Perhaps. Others may view this as the most compassionate way to deal with others. This is something you must decide. Your response says a lot more about you than the other person.

> ***Today I shall use compassion in dealing with difficult people.***

76: It's The Message Not The Messenger!

Several years ago a speaker friend of mine said, "It's the message not the messenger." At the time I had been in the speaking business for about five years and was concentrating all of my efforts into my presentation style—attempting to perfect that which I would call uniquely mine. His words fell on naïve ears. I wasn't ready to hear his journeyman advice: concentrate on the message.

I always respected this speaker because his message was so powerful. Therefore, his words about the message, not the messenger, stayed with me and incubated for years. At some point, I decided to revisit this issue. I began to focus more time and energy on what I had to say than how I would say it. I shelved the battle of style over substance.

Once I made this transition to focusing more on the message than the messenger interesting things happened. It got better: the message and my presentation of it. I focused on my real purpose for doing what I was doing: i.e. to share my experiences and knowledge. The emphasis shifted from theatrical gimmicks to proof sources that reinforced my message with credibility. It became more important to deliver a strong, relevant message than to focus primarily on delivery.

Curiously, my delivery got better because I invested

more energy and commitment in a stronger message. Natural enthusiasm and passion replaced the staged antics with which I had peppered my presentations. Spontaneity, variety, and conviction bolstered my message. Now I'm hired specifically for my message. It's a great message and I feel very privileged to be the one who delivers it.

Another dynamic has become more evident to me. When I was more concerned about the messenger, the focus was on me. It was all about me and the recognition for having delivered a great presentation. Now the emphasis is always on the message and the way it affects the group. I am no longer the centerpiece, just the fortunate guy who gets to do the presentation.

When we coach little league teams, isn't it for the children, not the parents? When we volunteer at church, it's the work that counts, not the credit we receive: although, recognition feels good. When I give you a present, isn't it more about your excitement than what an extraordinary gift-giver I am? If I have something to share with you—a gift or talent for singing, writing, or acting—isn't the real beauty in the expression and enjoyment of it? If I am a salesperson and I have a great product, isn't the sale always about how it benefits the customer?

Each of us has a message or gift of some kind. As we share it with other people, we must focus on the message. We achieve a depth that comes only from selfless giving. Subordinating yourself to your message breeds humility and invites the greatest respect from those who listen to you. You've transmitted your message by focusing on the receiver and not the sender. It's user-friendly and listener-oriented.

Simple Psychology

My friend who clued me in to this thinking tells an incredible story of human courage and spirit. He spent seven years as a Prisoner of War in the Hanoi Hilton. His name is Captain Gerry Coffee. He's written about this experience in his book, <u>Beyond Survival</u>. When he speaks you hear the details of a story; but more importantly, you begin to feel that within you is a story of your own personal courage and triumph. You walk away with a sense that you can do anything in this world you put your mind to. And Gerry does this by never losing sight of his mission: it's the message not the messenger.

What's your message to share?

Today I shall focus on my message to share with the world.

77: He Has A Good Heart

I was talking with my friend about the training business. He gave me a referral—the name of his friend who owns a newspaper. My friend thought our sales training courses could help his friend's sales force increase sales. My initial reaction was, "I really don't like the guy's politics and may find it difficult to distance my feelings if I did the work."

My friend responded, "He has a good heart!"

He caught me off-guard. I was embarrassed and ashamed of my willingness to prejudge this guy without having met him. I only knew what I had gotten second-hand through newspapers or word-of-mouth. What really irritated me was that I thought I was above this type of superficiality. He stunned me with his casual response. I failed to go beyond the obvious and look at what Martin Luther King described as "the content of his character."

Then I speculated, "How many others have I prejudged simply because I didn't like the packaging or the tone of their message?" "How many messages did I fail to hear because I didn't like the messenger?" And, "How many people have I dismissed because their thoughts challenged or threatened mine?"

Carl Rogers wrote, "It takes a great deal of inner strength and security to lose oneself in understanding another person . . . we risk being changed, even momentarily, as we listen to another's opinion." By opening ourselves to another's opinions, we risk changing our minds. And a mind challenged by the introduction of a new thought never returns to its original size.

"So, he has a good heart." I thought to myself. How would I know since I never took the time to understand him? Sosheki said, "Truth only reveals itself when one gives up all preconceived ideas."

What surprised me mostly was that I am in the open-mindedness business. I speak and write for a living. I share ideas with others, and I prejudged someone whom I never met based on rumor, innuendo, and things that appeared in his publication. It caused me to doubt if I would ever learn all the lessons life teaches.

So now the prescription for me is simple: listen with my heart; judge not the person; and challenge my intellect with the message.

And when I meet someone along the path of life whom I feel the need to dismiss immediately, I'll confront my bias with the question, "What's in his heart?"

Today as I interact with others, I shall look deeper into their hearts.

78: Don't Let Another's Opinion Hold You Back

There are significant people whose opinion we value: parents, teachers, coaches, friends, employees and bosses. In many cases, their opinions shape how we deal with the world. None of us lives in an opinion vacuum.

How important is another person's opinion to your self-esteem? How much influence are you willing to give someone else over your life? Will you let someone set your limits for you?

No one knows what's in your heart. They can speculate. No one feels the full impact of your determination. That's your call. No one can see inside your head. And, no one can tell you what's beyond your reach. You decide that for yourself. When it comes to limits, you set them and break them. You define you.

In 1980, I lost my voice to cancer. I underwent two surgeries to remove a tumor that was attached to my thyroid. Unfortunately, during the first operation my vocal chords were damaged. It reduced my rich baritone voice to a muted whisper. I could barely finish a sentence without being winded. I couldn't have a normal conversation in a moving automobile because the road noise overpowered my whisper. After six months of this frustration my doctor told me to prepare myself to go through life this way. Something deep inside me rejected his opinion. "How dare this man tell me to give up." I thought, "That's my call, not his!"

I found a speech therapist who worked with me three times a week for six months. She taught me to breathe differently—to generate enough wind to pass over my vocal chords. Every night I practiced the breathing and speaking exercises she prescribed. I set a goal for myself—to yell "Fore!" again on the golf course. Considering my golf game, I had a practical motive for this goal.

After several months of speech therapy, a tenant in my therapist's building asked her, "What are you guys doing in there, playing golf?" We knew the therapy was over.

In spite of my surgeon's opinion, I could now have a normal conversation. In our final session, my speech therapist said, "Tom, at first, when you came in here your vocal chords were so badly damaged, I never thought you would speak again; but I didn't have the heart to tell you!" Boy, am I thrilled she didn't. I may have believed her.

What a great lesson in life. When those around me told me I couldn't, I listened to my inner voice. It said, "Go for it." The bittersweet irony is that for the past fifteen years I have earned a living with my voice.

There's a beautiful irony inside you also. There's something you've always wanted to do; a place you wanted to visit; or a dream you wanted to pursue. One voice inside you says, "Forget it, that's not you. You're just not that kind of person." This is the collective voice of those who are looking out for you. Their motivation may be benign and sincere, but they don't know what's in your heart. They can't feel your passion. They can't understand the depths of your desire. And they sure as heck don't know your potential. That's your decision.

There's another voice in you. It's the voice of a dreamer, a zealot, and a winner. It's your voice of commitment and desire. This is the voice to hear. This is the beat of your drum. This is your potential calling. Answer the call. March to your drum beat. Listen to your inner voice yelling "Fore." The pay-off is tremendous. I know. I answered it!

Today I shall listen to and act on my inner voice.

79: What Others Teach Us

Being involved in education for most of my life, I'm interested in how people learn. If there's a better way to teach a skill, I want to hear about it. I'm also a realist. People need not sit in a classroom to learn. We learn from other people—not just trainers and teachers. As children we learn from parents. As parents we learn from children. And along the way, hopefully we're open enough to learn from each other.

Everyone with whom we interact teaches us something about life. Those whom we admire and respect show us the path to follow. They are role models, the winners, the successful real life heroes and heroines whose values and standards of behavior inspire us and give us direction.

Managers, peers, trainers, professors, employees, and friends teach us. They give us facts we can use, information to excel, and encourage us to stretch for the future. Mentors give us the principles of our profession to emulate. They teach us the dynamics of success. Our children teach us how we're doing as parents. Everyone teaches us something.

Mark Twain said, "God bless the failures in life for they teach us what not to do." You could write volumes of things to avoid by observing the people around you. Peers at work who struggle with their careers show you the path to avoid. Children vow to do a better job raising children than their parents. "When I become a manager, I'll never treat employees this way," says the disgruntled employee.

The ranting and raving of the opposing coach at a children's game reads like a primer of everything a coach should avoid. The inconsiderate neighbor who ought to be living on five isolated acres teaches us how not to live with others.

This became crystal clear to me as I listened to a driven, workaholic businessman describe his life. He enjoyed a frenetic travel schedule. He lived in hotels, worked seven days a week, and steamrolled anyone in his path. His marriage ended years ago. His friends were few, and his health questionable. He had amassed a small fortune but lost most of the meaning in his life. His one dimensional living was a glaring example of what most people hope to avoid in life. This was not a nice man.

Yogi Berra said, "Much can be observed by just watching." Everyone with whom we interact teaches us something. Our positive role models teach us what to do, how to work, and what to read. They are our pathfinders. They show us the paths to follow and walk with us for a while along the journey.

The failures also teach us something—what not to do. We watch what they read and don't read it. We observe how they work and avoid making the same mistakes. We observe their diets and eat differently. We experience how they treat others and vow never to act the same way. Mostly, we witness their priorities and thank our Creator for the wisdom to make better decisions.

Today, as you walk down the path of life, look for your teachers. They're there. They'll let you know if you're on the right path. Listen, watch, and learn. There are teachers and lessons everywhere.

Today I shall be open to the lessons of life.

Other Products by Tom Reilly

Books

- Value Added Customer Service™ $ 5.00
- Selling Smart™ $ 9.95
- Value Added Selling Techniques™ $19.95
- Value Added Sales Management™ $24.95

Cassettes

- Value Added Selling Techniques™ $49.99
  (4-cassette album)
- Communicative Selling Skills™ $59.99
  (6-cassette album)
- Relationship Selling™ $25.00
  (2-cassette album)

Courses and Speaking Topics

- Value Added Sales Management™
- Value Added Selling Techniques™
- There's No Traffic Jam on the Extra Mile!™
- Time and Territory Management
- Relationship Skills™
- Value Added Customer Service™
- Proactive Selling Techniques™

For Additional Information Contact:

Tom Reilly, President
Sales Motivational Services, Inc.
171 Chesterfield Industrial Boulevard
Chesterfield, Missouri 63005
314-537-3360